Socially ADDept™

A Manual for Parents of Children with ADHD and/or Learning Disabilities

Janet Z. Giler, Ph.D.

Publisher's Note

This publication is designed to provide accurate and authoritative information with regard to the subject matter covered. It is intended to help parents teach social skills to their children. For greater effect, children need to be in an *ADDept* Group facilitated by a trained, mental health professional. The author takes no responsibility for non-trained professionals leading *ADDept* groups.

Text and concept copyright ©2000 by Janet Z. Giler

Illustrations copyright ©1998

Edited by Julie Hanks Ph.D., Karl L. Metzenberg, Diane Wolf and Diane Billot

Cover Production: Cirrus Design

Cover Photography: Karl L. Metzenberg

Some images were obtained from IMSI's MasterClips Collection, 1895 Francisco Blvd. East, San Rafael, CA 94901-5506, USA

Printed in the United States of America

Published by

CES Publications
30 West Mission St. #5
Santa Barbara, CA 93101
(805) 563-2818

ISBN 0-9666969-2-1

Preface

Many children with ADHD and/or Learning Disabilities misunderstand or don't know the "hidden" rules of communication. Many parents don't know what to do when their children struggle with teasing or feelings of rejection. *Socially ADDept* helps children:

Comprehend and use appropriate body language

Handle teasing

Have increased self-awareness

Have increased respect for others

This book is not intended to be an introductory book on Learning Disabilities or ADHD. If you are just starting to consider if your child has these problems, please refer to Appendix A: What is Attention Deficit Hyperactivity Disorder? or Appendix B: What are Learning Disabilities? The references also list some excellent introductory books on these subjects. Many local libraries have videos on ADHD or Learning Disabilities that are worth seeing. Lastly, if you are on the internet, visit my parenting website, http://www.ld-add.com

Adept—thoroughly competent
ADDept™ is a trade name

Acknowledgments

I would like to thank the following people for their time, support, help and encouragement. Thanks go to: my husband Karl for his patience, editorial support and humor; my friends Julie Hanks, Diane Billot, Sonia Lane and Diane Wolf for their careful editing; Joan and Les Esposito of the Dyslexia Awareness and Resource Center for their support and encouragement; my son Conrad for allowing me to practice these techniques on him; and lastly, the children who attended my *ADDept* groups who have shown me which techniques work. However, this book would not have been written had I not understood a seminal concept that Richard Lavoie stated years ago; there is no way to compensate for poor social skills.

CONTENTS

Socially ADDept

Instructions for Parents

Social Skills Training for Children with ADHD or Learning Disabilities

Children with ADHD and Learning Disabilities often make social mistakes. They frequently mis-hear a communication, interrupt, answer out of turn, change the subject, misuse tone, misperceive the meaning of tone or intrude into another person's space. They are frequently the butt of jokes and USUALLY RESPOND AGGRESSIVELY to teasing. Because they have a difficult time ignoring teasing, they are an easy mark for more teasing. Many of their social errors can be prevented when children learn some basic social rules and skills.

Many of these children are classified as having Learning Disabilities because they process information differently. While many may receive help academically, we have tended to hope that they will learn social rules from other children. However, instead of learning, many continue to make the same mistakes because they don't know the rules of communication.

WHY SOCIAL SKILLS TRAINING?

1. LD/ADHD children don't know the rules of conversation
2. LD/ADHD children don't follow sequences
3. Conversations are sequential and operate by specific rules
4. LD/ADHD children frequently violate spatial boundaries of others
5. LD/ADHD children misperceive jokes
6. LD/ADHD children are frequently the butt of jokes
7. There is no way to compensate for poor social skills

Employers are more tolerant of problems related to job performance from processing inabilities than they are of social mistakes. In other words, since there is no way to compensate for poor social skills (there are ways to compensate for not being able to read , write or spell), we need to teach our children social skills as well as academic skills.

Many researchers have commented on the relationship between the LD children's perceptual problems and their social problems, noting that

3

LD and LD/ADHD children misperceive not only the content of a conversation, but also the impact of their responses and behavior on others. Instead of learning from their peers, they repeat the same social mistakes, leading to their being teased, rejected, or ignored by other children. Their social errors have profound effects on self-esteem and can lead to depression or disruptive behavior to gain attention. When children feel they cannot succeed in normal ways, they become disruptive, aggressive, and engage in bothersome behaviors. When socially rejected, they respond with increased hostility. Research indicates that 35% of LD students drop out of high school, and 31% of adolescents with Learning Disabilities will be arrested 3-5 years after high school. Up to 60% of the adolescents in treatment for substance abuse have Learning Disabilities. Since we know this population is at risk for aggression and hostility, higher drop-out rates, and drug and alcohol problems, it is imperative that we help these children master social skills that will enable them to succeed as adults. Lavoie (1994) has suggested that social skills are the one area of deficiency for which there are no compensation strategies. The success of these children depends entirely on their ability to master social interactions. Simple conversational rules such as cooperation, turn-taking, sequencing ideas, responding, understanding personal space and reading nonverbal cues are unknown to many LD/ADHD children.

Socially ADDept is designed to address the most common social errors made by LD/ADHD children: misreading body language, using tone inappropriately, violating others physical boundaries, perseverating on topics, and failing to show interest in others. The *ADDept Social Skills Curriculum* trains children to monitor themselves. It is a ten week program that teaches children to use ten essential social skills: (1) listening and responding, (2) showing interest by smiling and asking questions, (3) greeting others, (4) giving compliments, (5) understanding body language and vocal tones, (6) understanding personal space and appropriate touching, (7) joining an ongoing activity, (8) sharing and cooperating, (9) ignoring teasing, and lastly, (10) managing anger. To maximize benefits, this manual should be used in conjunction with the *ADDept* Curriculum.

Three Problem Areas for LD/ADHD Children

Among the various perceptual problems encompassed by the range of LD/ADHD categories, lack of perception regarding the effect one's behavior has upon others is most common. Research shows that LD/ADHD children frequently make mistakes in three areas: misinterpreting body language (kinesis); misusing

THREE PROBLEM AREAS FOR LD/ADHD CHILDREN

1. KINESIS — Inability to read facial expressions or body language
2. VOCALICS — Misinterpreting the use and meaning of pitch
3. PROXEMICS — Misunderstanding the use of personal space

pitch and misunderstanding its meaning (vocalics); and misunderstanding the rules of personal body space, frequently violating the space of others without being aware of the error (proxemics).

Language Difficulties and the Hidden Rules of Conversation

Many LD/ADHD children have problems with language. They may have difficulties with topic organization or they may fail to introduce the subject at all. They may perseverate on some detail without defining the main subject and then ignore the bored or uninterested verbal and nonverbal feedback they receive.

To have a conversation the speaker must attend to the listener's nonverbal feedback. Boredom or lack of interest can be read in the listener's facial expressions. LD/ADHD children may be so engrossed in talking, they fail to check if the person to whom they are speaking is interested. For example, LD/ADHD children with language difficulties may start talking about an experience such as skateboarding by describing in detail what the ramp looked like. After a minute or two of details on the ramp, they may or may not introduce the topic of

5

skateboarding. The confused and/or bored listener has long since stopped listening and is waiting for a chance to leave or change the topic. Many LD/ADHD children fail to notice the lack of interest and are surprised when the listener makes a derogatory comment. LD/ ADHD children usually do not understand why this happened.

> **SOCIAL PROBLEMS DUE TO LANGUAGE OR PERCEPTUAL SEQUENCING PROBLEMS**
>
> 1. Failure to introduce a topic clearly
> 2. Poor topic organization
> 3. Faulty sequencing
> 4. Failure to show interest when listening
> 5. Failure to read body language correctly
> 6. Failure to respect personal space

LD/ADHD children's perseveration (talking at length about a topic without attending to the interest of the listener) is seen by others as self-centeredness. When LD/ADHD children learn to respond to verbal or nonverbal feedback, they start correcting their behavior and become more aware of the needs of others.

Teaching LD/ADHD Children the Behaviors of Popular Children

In a study of popular children, Fox and Weaver found that popular children engage in the following behaviors when confronted with social situations: (1) they smiled and laughed with other children, (2) they greeted other children by name, (3) they initiated conversation by asking questions and showing interest, (4) they extended

> **SOCIAL BEHAVIORS OF POPULAR CHILDREN**
>
> 1. Smile and laugh
> 2. Greet others by name
> 3. Initiate conversations, ask questions, show interest
> 4. Extend invitations
> 5. Give compliments
> 6. Share
> 7. Have a good appearance

invitations to others, (5) they gave compliments, (6) they shared, and (7) they paid attention to their appearance. While previous training methods have focused on teaching LD/ADHD children to avoid annoying or problematic behaviors, teaching children how to use positive behaviors is more effective. The *ADDept* Curriculum teaches pro-social behaviors.

Two Major Types of Social Skills Deficits

There are two major groups of children with social skills deficits, children with acquisition or performance problems. Different training methods need to be utilized in order to train each group successfully. Gresham and Elliott (1994) have noted that there are children with acquisition deficits who do not have sufficient information on the mechanics of performing a skill or the information to judge when such a skill is appropriate. These children respond well to teaching methods that use direct instruction, modeling, behavior rehearsal, and coaching.

Impulsive Children have **performance** problems; they know the mechanics of how to perform the skills but they have trouble because of their inability to master self-

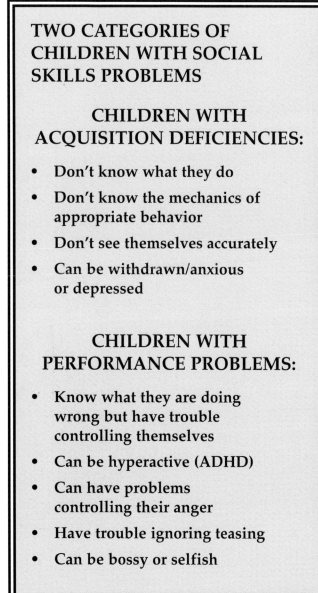

TWO CATEGORIES OF CHILDREN WITH SOCIAL SKILLS PROBLEMS

CHILDREN WITH ACQUISITION DEFICIENCIES:

- Don't know what they do
- Don't know the mechanics of appropriate behavior
- Don't see themselves accurately
- Can be withdrawn/anxious or depressed

CHILDREN WITH PERFORMANCE PROBLEMS:

- Know what they are doing wrong but have trouble controlling themselves
- Can be hyperactive (ADHD)
- Can have problems controlling their anger
- Have trouble ignoring teasing
- Can be bossy or selfish

control. Children with performance deficits can judge when and how to implement the skill. They do not benefit from programs that teach them how to acquire new skills. Their problems are due to issues such as anxiety, impulsivity, or aggressiveness. The methods that work with these children include reprimands, time-out, and clear "if-then" consequences. Children who have primary problems with impulsivity or aggressiveness cannot fully benefit from the *ADDept* method until their impulsivity is brought under control which usually can be accomplished through behavioral therapy or the use of appropriate medications (See Appendix C).

LD with Attention Deficit Hyperactivity Disorder[1]

Socially ADDept and the *ADDept* Curriculum were created to meet the acquisition needs of the LD and LD/ADHD child. A conservative estimate is that twenty-five percent of LD children also have Attention Deficit Hyperactivity Disorder. Some professionals believe that the figure is closer to fifty percent and may present more in the Inattentive subgroup.

ADHD, according to the DSM IV (*Diagnostic and Statistical Manual*, Fourth Edition, 1994) has three major forms, the Inattentive and Impulsive type, the Hyperactive/Impulsive type and the Mixed group, Hyperactive and Impulsive. People with all types of ADD/ADHD display these following six characteristics:

1. Short attention span

2. Distractibility

3. Impulsive behavior

4. Free flight of ideas

5. Poor organizational skills

6. Insatiability

---

1 The official name was changed from ADD to ADHD. ADD or ADHD refers to all forms of Attention Deficit Disorder.

In addition to these six characteristics, children with Attention Deficit Hyperactivity Disorder exhibit hyperactive characteristics.

How ADHD Affects the Brain

What are the origins of ADHD? Simply stated, the brains of individuals with ADHD function differently. Many researchers have noted the frontal cortex functions more slowly, and less glucose is metabolized in the prefrontal cortex.

At a 1997 national medical symposium on neuroimaging in Learning Disabilities and Developmental Disorders, MRI and PET scans showed differences in the frontal cortex region of the brain. While these neuroimaging techniques are still experimental, they indicate that there are physical, neurological causes for ADHD.

One way to describe this slowing of brain activity is to say the brain functions too slowly while processing sensory information. This means the child or adult fails to sort and store sensory stimuli. So when the stimulation level is low, the child or adult can focus well, even hyper-focus. But, put the same person in a room filled with noise or activity, and they become increasingly stimulated by the amount of sensory information they receive. They are unable to filter it out or process it fast enough.

New research indicates that this failure to limit or store sensory information may be due to increased levels of dopamine in the caudate, an area of the brain that is responsible for putting on the brain's brakes. This increase of dopamine is thought to slow down the braking mechanism.

To make the diagnosis of Attention Deficit Hyperactivity Disorder, the major symptoms of impulsivity, inattention and/or hyperactivity should be present BEFORE THE AGE OF 7 and be observed in at least two environments, school and home. If a child is impulsive at home but not at school (or vice versa), there is probably a different reason for the impulse problem.

The child diagnosed with ADHD Inattentive type, with or without Learning Disabilities, can be an excellent candidate for **ADDept** training. As is true for LD children, ADHD children also have missed learning social rules due to their inattention. These children benefit from the direct instruction and self-evaluation components of **ADDept** training.

If the primary problem is impulse control, the teacher and parents need to set up a behavioral contract that has clearly defined consequences and rewards. Impulsive children frequently need to be referred to a physician for a medical evaluation.

Children with primary impulse problems benefit from a behavioral management program that includes:

1. Parent education

2. Behavior contracting with clear, positive and negative consequences. Adults need to provide consistent and immediate consequences (e.g. loss of privileges) when children do not follow directions or act inappropriately.

3. Medication evaluation

Basic Social Skills

There are 10 basic social competency clusters in **Socially ADDept** and the **ADDept** Curriculum. Greeting, listening and responding are critical skills that make up the first cluster of skills. These skills are utilized in all subsequent lessons. Listening is part of a feedback loop. The listener needs to hear the words and also needs to respond to the speaker verbally or nonverbally. Many LD/ADHD children fail to complete the feedback loop; they fail to ask questions, make comments, give compliments, or show interest nonverbally. In essence, they fail to acknowledge that they have heard the speaker. In the first lesson of the **ADDept** Curriculum, children practice verbal and nonverbal ways of acknowledging the speaker.

The second cluster focuses on understanding nonverbal communication. As stated earlier, many of the mistakes made by LD/ADHD children fall into this category (kinesis and proxemics). Since almost sixty percent of communication is nonverbal, many social problems result from misreading or ignoring the nonverbal message. Whereas the verbal message communicates content, the nonverbal message conveys the emotional tone of the speaker. If listeners are interested in a person but fail to show interest through gestures, tone, or words, the speaker usually "feels" they don't care about him/her. The ability to interpret and use facial expression, posture, gestures and tone is essential to good communication.

Another goal is for children to understand what it means when the words and tone disagree. Many jokes rely on the listener perceiving the incongruity between the verbal and nonverbal message. This is confusing to many LD/ADHD children who are very literal; they listen to the verbal message and ignore the tone. Because of this, they miss the contradiction of the words and the tone which is what frequently makes jokes funny.

Many conflicts arise when children fail to respect the culturally agreed upon rules of personal space. Many ADHD/LD children do not know what the agreed upon boundaries are, so they get too close, or they take or touch someone else's property without permission. When others react to the invasion of their personal space, LD/ADHD children are dumfounded. They literally do not know they have violated someone's space. Defining what the culturally accepted personal boundaries are helps LD/ADHD children behave more appropriately.

Other lessons focus on interacting skills, including the proper way to join an ongoing activity. Most LD/ADHD children do not know to wait to be invited to join the activity. Because they don't take time or they misperceive body language, they don't know if the children are giving them friendly or unfriendly signals (referred to as STOP signs). Also addressed are sharing and cooperation. Many children with ADHD/LD need to recognize and reduce their bossy behaviors.

Teasing is a problem for many LD/ADHD children who frequently get in trouble for responding aggressively. Parents are encouraged to role-play the new methods that are suggested in Lesson Seven, "Dealing with Teasing."

11

Ten Essential Social Skills

Socially ADDept and the *ADDept Social Skills Curriculum* covers ten basic social skills:

1. Greeting others

2. Listening and responding

3. Showing interest by smiling and asking questions

4. Giving compliments

5. Understanding body language and vocal tones

6. Understanding personal space and appropriate touching

7. Learning to join an ongoing activity

8. Sharing and cooperating

9. Ignoring teasing

10. Managing anger

TEN ESSENTIAL SOCIAL SKILLS

1. Greeting others
2. Listening and responding
3. Showing interest
4. Giving compliments
5. Understanding body language and tone of voice
6. Comprehending personal space and appropriate touching
7. Joining ongoing activities with peers
8. Sharing and cooperating
9. Handling teasing
10. Managing anger

The Parents' Role

Parents of children with LD/ADHD often find it difficult to teach social skills. Many of these children do not learn from others' modeling the appropriate behavior. It doesn't matter if the parents have good table manners or good interactions with their friends. Their children may not copy their actions. That is because many ADHD/LD children have nonverbal problems. They need specific instructions about what to do and why they should do it.

Opportunistic Reinforcement

Parents have the unique opportunity to see their children interact in a variety of different situations. This can be painful as well as rewarding, depending on the parents' expectations and patience.

Parents are encouraged to use these communication methods to support new behaviors.

Communication Methods

1. Use humor
2. Use self-disclosure
3. Model making mistakes
4. Reframe the problem
5. Prescribe the symptom
6. Coach the children on desirable behaviors
7. Ignore mistakes
8. Restate or identify behaviors observed
9. Ask clarifying questions
10. Punctuate change to draw attention to new, positive behaviors
11. Use praise

Using Humor to Recuperate from Mistakes

One of the best ways to help LD/ADHD children change is to support and correct them simultaneously. Humor can be both corrective and supportive at the same time. One can use humor to exaggerate a mistake so it becomes absurd. When children interrupt, parents might take their behavior of interrupting and continuously interrupting them, exaggerating what interrupting looks like. Since this is a form of teasing, it should only be done if the children will not be hurt by it. If they cannot laugh at their mistakes, this is not a strategy that parents should use.

If children cannot laugh at themselves, parents need to help them find ways to make some of their mistakes funny. People who learn to laugh at their mistakes often become very successful adults. They have learned an important lesson: everybody makes mistakes.

> ## Use Humor to Recuperate from an Embarrassing Mistake

Frequently children with LD/ADHD stop conversations to point out a mistake that they have made. This interruption breaks the flow of conversation and other children or adults then focus on the mistake and don't know what to say. All children need to have recuperation strategies that don't interrupt the flow of conversation. One way is to ignore the mistake. If children need to call attention to their mistakes, it is best if they do it with humor as it makes others more comfortable.

Dr. Mel Levine, the keynote speaker at the 1999 DARC Conference (Dyslexia Awareness and Resource Center) said that as children, our mistakes seem horrendous. As adults, many of us have turned our mistakes into positive traits. We do this through learning to laugh about them because what we can laugh about we can accept in ourselves. Adults who can laugh at themselves usually have positive self-esteem. They know their positive and negative traits and accept that they make mistakes.

Children with LD/ADHD may not have lots of confidence in themselves. It is important for parents to help their children recognize their positive and negative traits. A very positive way to learn to accept mistakes is for parents to model making mistakes while laughing at themselves. By showing children that you accept your own mistakes, you also teach them that it is okay for them to make mistakes. This is an important recuperation strategy. Parents can also use self-disclosure to show their children how they were able to make the transition from thinking their mistakes were terrible to seeing them as humorous.

Preparation

The parents' role involves coaching, overseeing and preparation.

Prepare Children for the New Situation

Since most children with LD/ADHD do not like change, any transition to a new situation can be difficult. New situations can be frightening and some children may avoid doing new things. To help reduce anxiety, parents can take their children to visit a new school, camp, or after-school activity before they start. If possible, make contact with another child who is in the new school or camp. Parents might talk to the principal or camp director to explain that they know that their son or daughter may need a little extra help in making a transition.

Prepare the New Situation for Your Children

Parents also need to make clear to schools or camps, what their children's particular needs are. As an example, a mother told the Boy Scout leader that her son was dyslexic. It didn't occur to her that the scout leader didn't know what dyslexia was. She was horrified to watch her son struggling to read a passage in front of all the assembled parents and children. Parents need to be very specific and tell people, "Please do not have my son read out loud."

Prepare Children for Recess

Recess and other unstructured times are difficult for many LD/ADHD children. During these times, their inability to read and respond to social cues is more pronounced. Recess can also be a particularly painful time for children who are not coordinated or good at sports.

LD/ADHD children may need coaching on how to join ongoing activities. Many ADHD children seek to be the center of attention. They don't join groups; they intrude upon them and change the activity, the conversation, and certainly the group's focus (Lesson Six, "Joining an Ongoing Group.")

Children need to be encouraged to make friends with a shy person or someone who doesn't have a lot of friends. Parents may also need to encourage them to come up with an activity that they can do by themselves or with one or two other children such as drawing, reading, computer games, going to the library or helping teachers out in the room. Some children excel in drama, music or art and should be encouraged to join in group or after school activities.

Helping Clumsy Children

Cratty (1993) has estimated that 30–50 percent of children with Learning Disabilities have coordination apraxia (meaning they have trouble coordinating their muscle movements). This is particularly painful for children who want to play team sports. These children may wish to join in a team sport but the other members of the team may not want to let them join because they see these children as hampering their ability to win. Parents can help their children by giving them other activities that do not involve gross motor coordination or encourage them to do activities that specifically train gross motor coordination.

Many boys with (and without) LD/ADHD gravitate towards computer and videogames. They like being in the fantasy realm in which they are able to conquer the demons and be the master. There is some benefit to videogames; they can improve eye-hand coordination. While some degree of this activity maybe useful, parents need to make sure that their children do not play video games to the exclusion of interacting with others.

Parents can help children find an activity in which they can excel. For some, it will be music or art. For others it may be martial arts, hiking or mountain biking. Many older children enjoy swimming, fishing, surfing, diving, golfing, and skiing. Many of these activities can be shared with other children, because there isn't the same level of group cooperation or team coordination necessary to succeed. Another benefit is that these activities can be shared with children of all ages as well as adults.

Children who have coordination problems can be helped by therapies (sports or martial arts) that focus on coordinating the sensory-motor system. Ayers (1972) developed a system called sensory-motor integration that specifically targets balance and coordination problems. Sensory-motor integration is usually done by a physical therapist or an occupational therapist. Adaptive physical education can be useful.

The Parents' Role in Planning Social Activities

Parents have a large role in planning and monitoring social activities for children. For younger children (below the age of 10), the parent can plan the activity or help the children plan the activity. The parent needs to be available to monitor activities. As children get older, they need to learn how to be responsible for planning their own activities. It is very difficult (if not impossible) to plan activities for teenagers.

The Initial Social Contact

The initial social contact between two children should be a fairly structured activity. It should also be a shorter period e.g. less than two hours. CHADD (Children and Adults with ADD) recommends that the initial activity be more structured, such as a trip to a playground, museum, or an activity such as seeing a movie or going to play miniature golf or bowling. If the children have a special interest in common, the play period should include this activity. The goal is to have the visitor want to come back and play again. Better to end the visit earlier and on a positive note.

Monitoring Play

Parents should monitor play until they are sure that the children are getting along. Even when children are getting along, parents will still need to intervene and correct inappropriate behavior when there is any type of physical aggression or unkind remarks. Tone and space violations should be dealt with after the visitor leaves unless parents hear the other child complain or ask their child to stop a behavior and their child has disregarded the request to stop. It is appropriate to give children time-out even when another child is visiting or to use short breaks when the children get too excited.

Take breaks when children get *too* stimulated

Praise children often for positive interactions

Parents should also monitor their children's play for positive behaviors.

The play period is a great time to give positive praise when parents notice:

- Sharing

- Friendly play

- Kind remarks

Dealing with Perseveration

Many children with LD/ADHD perseverate on details instead of introducing a topic clearly. When children speak for over 45 seconds and parents cannot determine what the topic is, parents need to give them a signal that the listener is lost. Parents need to agree upon a signal with their children such as holding up 10 fingers, that lets them know that the listeners are not following their story. Parents need to encourage their children to start over and introduce the topic clearly.

Parents need to explain to their children that when people don't follow what they are talking about, the person listening will "space out," change the topic, or leave. Some children tease the speaker when they can't follow the topic. Many parents unfortunately, pretend to listen when they are not interested. Parents are embarrassed that they aren't listening, so instead of telling their children that they are lost or not interested, they just pretend to listen. This doesn't help children learn how to judge their audience and respond appropriately. Parents need to teach children what to do when people aren't listening. Should they keep talking or should they stop and ask a question?

Table Manners

Many children and adults with ADHD/LD have poor table manners. Many eat with their mouths open, talk with their mouths full of food, or in general, eat messily. While poor table manners may not be an issue with their peers when they are younger, it will be a problem for them as they mature. You have been in situations with adults who talk with their mouths full and never said a word to them. You may have thought twice about wanting to share another meal with them. Since neatness is a trait of popular children, it is important for parents to make sure their children know and use good table manners.

Since many children seem to go on automatic pilot when they eat, a simple strategy is to put a mirror in view so they can see themselves during the meal. Reward them for positive table manners such as:

- Not talking with their mouth full

- Using utensils properly

- Using simple phrases such as "please" and "thank you"

Charting Negative Behavior

There are children who are very impulsive and persistently engage in negative behaviors. Many are unaware that they are behaving in an annoying fashion. These children need additional support from their parents and teachers to chart incidents of annoying behaviors such as interrupting, making noise, failing to respect someone's space, or namecalling. This chart can be used to record these behaviors.

Behavior	*Mon*	*Tues*	*Wed*	*Thurs*	*Fri*	*Sat*	*Sun*
Interrupting							
Making Noises							
Space Violations							
Name-Calling							

Helping Children Who Are Poor Problem Solvers

A difficult task for parents is to help their children who do not solve problems well or who do not perceive the mistakes they have made. There are four principles that parents need to keep in mind:

FEEDBACK

EMPATHY

SELF-PERCEPTION

ALTERNATIVE BEHAVIORS

Frequently, children do not see the social mistakes they have made. The first step in giving feedback is to check and see if the children recognize that they have made an error. If so, do they know what these errors are? Parents need to listen to their children's concept of the problem. Parents then need to make sure they heard them correctly. For children who do not understand their own errors, parents need to role-play the errors with them.

Teaching Empathy

A goal in role-playing interactions is to show children how it felt to be on the receiving end of the aggressive, bossy, or hurtful behavior. After the role-play is over, ask, "How did that feel?"

Many children are so busy being impulsive or considering their own feelings that they haven't taken time to focus on how the other person feels. Since being considerate of other's feeling is one of the key factors in what makes people friends, acquiring this skill is very important for your children.

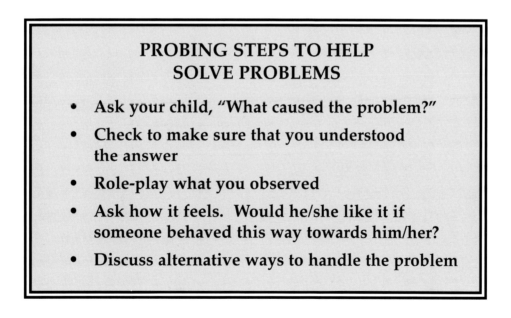

**PROBING STEPS TO HELP
SOLVE PROBLEMS**

- **Ask your child, "What caused the problem?"**
- **Check to make sure that you understood the answer**
- **Role-play what you observed**
- **Ask how it feels. Would he/she like it if someone behaved this way towards him/her?**
- **Discuss alternative ways to handle the problem**

Role-play Alternative Methods

After children have some grasp of their error, ask them to help come up with better ways to respond. If children cannot come up with alternatives, parents can give suggestions. The last step is for parents to role-play the new behavior with their children.

Parents of adolescents need to know that adolescents will "tune out" anything that sounds like a "lecture." Unless adolescents specifically ask for help, parents are better off sharing their own experiences, e.g. how they handled a similar situation. Parents need to remind themselves that the major task for adolescents is to figure out solutions for themselves.

Meeting Other Parents

Parent meetings offer the opportunity to meet and hear about the problems and successes that other parents of ADHD/LD children experience. Parents usually feel better meeting other parents who are having similar problems raising their children. It helps them to feel less isolated and more normal. Parents should attempt to join a local group. CHADD, a national support group for parents whose children have ADHD, has chapters in most large cities in the United States. Parents can contact CHADD for the listing of their local chapter.

HOW TO USE THIS BOOK

The following lessons are broken up into two major parts. The regular text contains a general discussion of the topics being presented. The charts summarize the major points of the topic.

The indented, italicized text is suggested dialogue to use with your child and contains questions to ask. If your child doesn't know the answer (s), use the suggested answers found below the questions to explain the topic.

The lessons include exercises for your child to do (with your assistance) and are noted by ★ or as numbered homework exercises.

LESSON ONE:

Friendship Skills and Setting Goals

LESSON ONE: Friendship Skills and Setting Goals

Children don't usually think about what qualities make people friends. They only pay attention to the fact that they have friends or that they aren't friends with someone anymore. Frequently, they don't know why someone stopped being friends with them. In this lesson, the parents ask their children what are the skills that people use to make and keep friends. The italicized text contains suggested discussions for parents to have with their children. In these discussions, we cover the ten essential friendship skills. This lesson introduces the idea that making and keeping friends is a skill that children can learn.

We are here to learn friendship skills.

Do you know what friendship skills are?

Can you name some friendship skills?

What do you like about your friends?

What do you like to do with your friends?

Parents write down what their children say.

Parents reiterate or add the following:

We like children who:

- *Care about us*

- *Play with us*

- *Listen to us*

- *Share with us*

- *Laugh at our jokes*

★ Do **Exercise 1: Friendly People Do**

EXERCISE 1: Friendly People Do

Think about the popular children in your school class. What do they do that makes people like them? It turns out that friendly people do some things in common. Can you guess what friendly people do?

- *Do they greet you and smile?*

- *Do they ask you how your day is?*

- *Do they listen to you when you talk?*

Place a check next to the following situations if you think the person was being friendly or not being friendly.

A person passes you on the street and looks you in the eye and smiles and nods?

     ❏   Friendly   ❏   Not Sure   ❏   Unfriendly

You see a kid you know, and he looks sad. You go over to talk to him.

     ❏   Friendly   ❏   Not Sure   ❏   Unfriendly

When you see someone you know, you say "hi" quickly and look away.

     ❏   Friendly   ❏   Not Sure   ❏   Unfriendly

When a friend wants to tell you about a new game, you change the subject because you are jealous.

     ❏   Friendly   ❏   Not Sure   ❏   Unfriendly

A child in your class brings his/her dog to school. You go over and ask questions such as "Can I pet him?"

     ❏   Friendly   ❏   Not Sure   ❏   Unfriendly

Discuss this list of ten friendship skills with your children. By introducing the concept of friendship making skills, parents begin the process of empowering children: making friends is a skill. Children can acquire new skills; it just takes practice.

Ten Friendship Skills

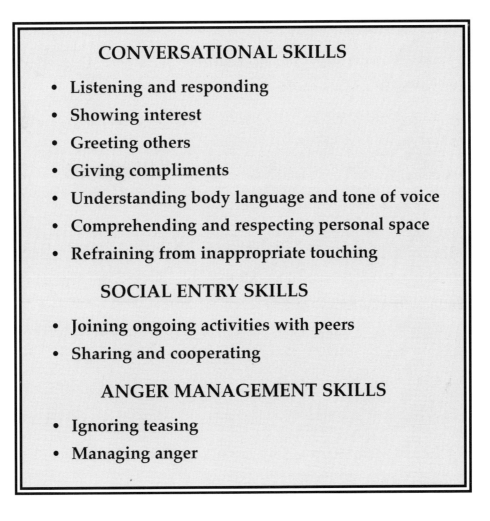

CONVERSATIONAL SKILLS

- Listening and responding
- Showing interest
- Greeting others
- Giving compliments
- Understanding body language and tone of voice
- Comprehending and respecting personal space
- Refraining from inappropriate touching

SOCIAL ENTRY SKILLS

- Joining ongoing activities with peers
- Sharing and cooperating

ANGER MANAGEMENT SKILLS

- Ignoring teasing
- Managing anger

Our goal is to increase your skills in these areas.

Do you want to learn how to make more friends?

Would you like to learn how to handle teasing?

From this conversation, parents help their children construct goals.

Write down the goals that your children set for themselves using this form.

Here are some possible goals from which to choose:

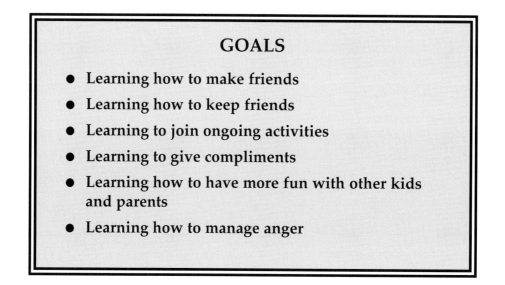

GOALS

- Learning how to make friends
- Learning how to keep friends
- Learning to join ongoing activities
- Learning to give compliments
- Learning how to have more fun with other kids and parents
- Learning how to manage anger

Which skills would you like to work on developing?

★ Do Exercise 2: Defining My Personal Goals (see page 34).

Define Positive Qualities

We all have qualities that we like about ourselves but we have been taught if we tell people what we like about ourselves, it will be thought of as bragging. I want you to do a little internal bragging this week. I want you to create a list of things that you like about yourself. At the end of this lesson, there is an exercise called Tooting My Horn: Creating Positive Self-talk. Please feel free to brag about yourself to yourself or to your family.

We all talk to ourselves. Sometimes this self-talk is negative, and we criticize ourselves for what we didn't do well. Negative self-talk can become a bad habit. As part of our work in these lessons, I want to help you create some good habits. One of these habits is positive self-talk. It's important to say good things to yourself.

Ask for examples of some positive affirmations. Then introduce and review **Chart: Positive Affirmations**.

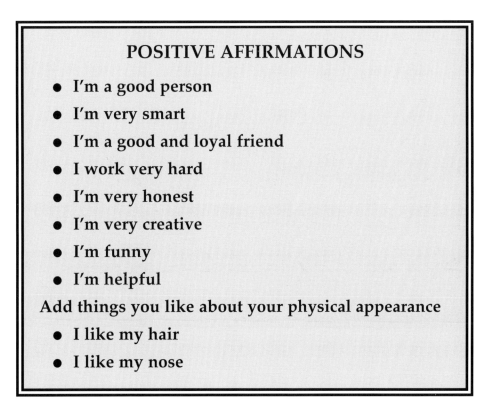

POSITIVE AFFIRMATIONS

- I'm a good person
- I'm very smart
- I'm a good and loyal friend
- I work very hard
- I'm very honest
- I'm very creative
- I'm funny
- I'm helpful

Add things you like about your physical appearance

- I like my hair
- I like my nose

Other qualities can also be added to your list, such as activities that you do well, for example, athletics, making friends, cooking, arts and crafts, writing or creative talents. If you get stuck, think of all the things you like about your best friend. Many times, you like people who are similar to you.

This list of personal qualities isn't a list that you need to share with other people. This is a list to keep and share with yourself, particularly if you are feeling badly. It's a list to remind you of all the wonderful things you have to offer.

For some children, you need to make sure they understand the distinction between what they say to themselves (positive self-talk) and what they should share with others (bragging).

Children with ADHD/LD: A Different Kind of Mind

Some positive qualities that your children may possess are:

- Rapid grasp of concepts

- Awareness of patterns

- Energy

- Curiosity

- Concentration on applied tasks when interested

- Exceptional memory for certain details

- Empathy

- Vulnerability/openness

- Heightened sensory perceptions

- Divergent thinking

Listening

One of the most important Friendship Skills is listening.

What are some of the things good listeners do?

Parents write down the answers, then introduce and review their child's comments.

Chart: Listening

LISTENING

- Face the person
- Make eye contact
- Think about what others are saying

Many children know how to listen passively. What they don't know how to do is be good, active listeners.

Active Listening

The first part of listening is to show positive interest by using good body language and tracking what the person is saying. The second part of listening is to let the person know that you heard them.

What are ways that you let someone know that you heard them?

Answer: *Asking Questions*

Asking questions is a great way to let someone know you are following them and are interested in what they are saying. Many questions start with the words: Who, Why, What, When, Where?

What else can we do to show we are listening?

Answer: *Restating*

Another good way to show interest is to restate what the person said. So, you liked how the movie ended?

Reward your child anytime you notice them:

- Making GOOD eye contact

- Attending to what someone is saying

- Showing interest nonverbally

- Listening without interrupting

Rewards can include:

- Verbal praise such as "I liked when you did . . ."

- Touching

- Nonverbal body signal (thumbs up, high five, a smile)

Dealing with Perseveration

Many LD/ADHD children perseverate. It's as though they get stuck on the small details and go into elaborate descriptions without introducing the topic clearly or checking to see if the person is interested. Many of these children will talk for more than 45 seconds without clearly identifying the topic so the listener cannot follow what they are saying. Most parents have learned to just "tune out" their children or to ask them questions to redirect them.

Most people, including parents, don't tell children when they perseverate, ramble, or fail to introduce a topic clearly. Actually, one minute is longer than most people are willing to listen when they can't follow a conversation. When they aren't able to follow, most people wait quietly for a chance to ask a question, change the conversation or politely depart. Some people are not polite and just interrupt or withdraw or tease the person when they can't follow the topic.

The way we suggest handling perseveration is to make a deal with your children. You agree beforehand that when you are not following what they are saying or are not interested in this topic, you will give them a signal that means, "Take ten seconds and observe my interest level." Children need to recognize when they are "rambling" and also, when their listener isn't interested or engaged in listening. Two basic recovery strategies are recommended: (1) introduce the topic more clearly or (2) change the subject by asking a question that engages the other person.

Sometimes I get lost while you are talking. I want to make a deal with you that if I'm lost or not listening, I will give you a sign. When I give you this sign it means that I want you to take ten seconds to introduce the main topic or change the topic.

Parents can make it a game. Reward children for recognizing non-interested body language and behaving appropriately. When children perseverate, other people tune them out. Unfortunately, if they do it a lot, people start to anticipate a negative experience and start to avoid them or actually tell them to "shut up."

Work out a signal with your children so they see when they lose your attention. Instruct them to take a few deep breaths, focus on the most important point, and say it in one sentence.

Homework for children:

- Do Exercise 2 and 3 together

- Work out a signal for perseveration

- Practice listening

Homework for parents:

- Name three qualities you like about your child.

- Name three things that you do well as a parent.

- Look for positive things to say to your child.

  Repeat often.

EXERCISE 2: Defining My Personal Goals

Circle appropriate goals or add your own

      to make friends

      to keep friends

      to join ongoing activities

      to give compliments

      to have more fun

      to manage teasing

to _____

_____

to _____

_____

to _____

_____

EXERCISE 3: Tooting My Horn

You possess qualities that you like about yourself. These qualities are the basis of self-esteem. This exercise asks you to define your personal positive qualities. Here are examples of positive qualities (called positive affirmations).

Circle the ones that fit you:

- I'm a good person

- I'm very smart

- I'm a good and loyal friend

- I work very hard

- I'm very honest

- I'm very creative

- I'm funny

- I'm helpful

Add things you like about your physical appearance:

- I like my hair

- I like my nose

Now make your own list:

_____

_____

_____

_____

_____

_____

LESSON TWO:

Conversational Skills

LESSON TWO: Conversational Skills — Being a Good Listener

Listening

Most people spend about 55% of their time listening. Of the four basic communication skills, listening is one of the most important skills we can master. If you don't know how to listen, you can't have a conversation. LD/ADHD children frequently (1) fail to listen without interrupting, (2) do not acknowledge they have heard what the speaker said, (3) respond by changing the conversation, or (4) respond by talking about themselves. The steps to having a good conversation are:

- Listening

- Responding by using appropriate body language and eye contact

- Asking questions

The most important conversational skill is listening. Most people think of listening as a fairly passive activity, but a big part of listening involves closing the feedback loop and letting the person know they have been heard.

Why is it important to listen?

Some answers are:

- *For directions*

- *To learn*

- *To be friendly*

- *To show someone you care*

How do you listen?

Ask your child to listen to you as you speak for 30 seconds to one minute. Ask your child to face you and to demonstrate good listening skills.

Identify what you observed.

Chart: Body Language of Listening

> **BODY LANGUAGE OF LISTENING**
>
> **STOP!**   Pay attention to the speaker
>
> **LOOK**   at the speaker — Eye Contact
>
> **LEAN**   FORWARD slightly towards the speaker
>
> **THINK**   about what the speaker is saying

How Do You Show Someone You Are Listening?

Listening is a two-part process. First you have to attend to the words and then you have to let the speaker know that you have heard and understood what he/she is saying.

How do you let the person know you heard them?

Write down responses:

- *Look at the person*

- *Lean forward*

- *Nod*

Demonstrate the body language of boredom. Ask your child:

Am I listening? How did you know?

Write down the negative behaviors that showed that you are not listening:

- *Looking away*

- *Leaning away from you*

- *Grimacing and making faces*

- *Rolling your eyes*

- *Looking down*

Listening Mistakes

Let's demonstrate the wrong way of listening.

Ask your child to be the listener. Ask him/her to make as many mistakes as possible while he/she is listening.

Ask your child to interrupt, look away, or change the subject. When you have completed this exercise, ask your child:

What did you do wrong?

You can write it down or restate it. Make sure to include these body language errors:

- *Looked away*

- *Looked bored*

- *Leaned away*

- *Interrupted*

There is another way children fail to show interest. It involves what they say or fail to say to the person who is speaking.

What you can say or do that shows the person you aren't interested in their conversation?

If your child has trouble identifying these behaviors, you can demonstrate listening the wrong way:

- Change the topic
- Talk about yourself
- Say nothing
- Interrupt

Ask your child to show you how to listen the right way.

Show me how you listen when you do it the right way.

Listening Has Two Parts

We show interest nonverbally through our:

- Eyes
- Facial expression
- Body gestures

> **ACTIVE LISTENING: Nonverbal ways of attending:**
>
> - Nod head in agreement or disagreement
> - Make guttural sounds such as Uh huh, Um, etc.

ACTIVE LISTENING: Verbal Ways of Responding:

- Questions for more information:
  "I don't get what you mean, will you explain it?"

- Paraphrasing: "I heard you say that the sky was yellow this morning, is that what you meant to say?"

- Making comments: "I see what you mean."

- Giving compliments: "That's cool."

We ask questions to try and get more information, such as,

"I don't get what you mean, will you explain it?"

Some examples of verbal ways of showing listening are:

- Questions — asking for more information

- Statements — about content

- Compliments — "gee that's cool"

Paraphrasing questions shows the speaker that we heard their words, but we aren't sure about the meaning. Paraphrasing can also be a way of asking for more information.

EXERCISE 4: Listening Facts

Here are some things to think about when you listen:

- What is the speaker saying?

- Do I understand what he/she means?

- Do their words and their body language agree?

- How do I show that I am interested?

In this picture, is the boy who is listening showing that he is interested or bored?

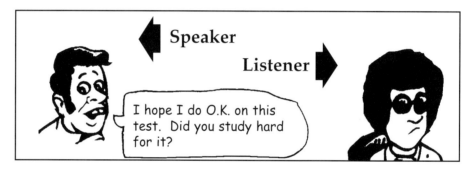

Is the girl listening and interested? How can you tell?

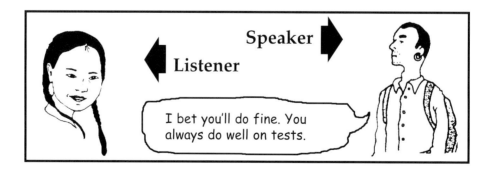

EXERCISE 5: Eye Contact

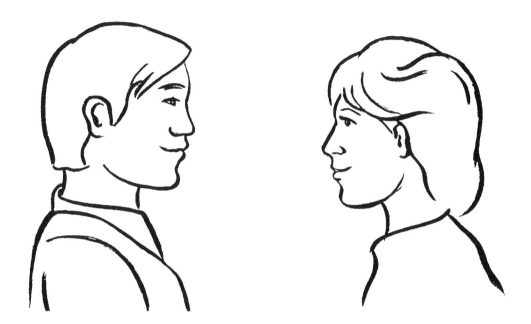

Why is it important to have good eye contact?

Do people think you are listening if you don't look at them?

Is this true in all cultures?

Give two examples of times you can't have good eye contact.

1.

2.

EXERCISE 6: It's Those Eyes!

James avoids eye contact with everyone. He keeps his head down and looks away when someone is talking to him.

How does it feel to talk to James?

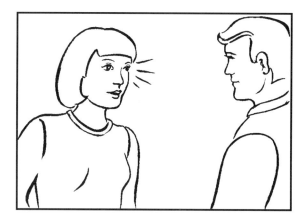

Nancy stares when she talks.

How do you feel when someone stares at you?

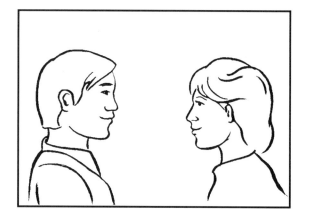

Mike makes you feel good when he looks at you. He looks as he listens, and his eyes show you he is interested.

How does it feel to talk to Mike?

LESSON THREE:

Verbal Conversational Skills

LESSON THREE: Verbal Conversational Skills

In the last lesson, we talked about paying attention nonverbally. We talked about the importance of eye contact, gestures and body posture. We also practiced listening and asking questions.

What are two parts of a conversation?

> **Answer:** listening and responding

How much time do we spend listening?

> **Answer:** 55%

Practice Asking Questions

We are going to discuss how we participate verbally in conversations by asking questions, making comments, giving compliments, and recognizing the importance of tone to communicate how we feel.

ACTIVE LISTENING

NONVERBAL WAYS OF ATTENDING:

- Nodding head in agreement or disagreement
- Making acknowledging sounds such as "Uh huh"

VERBAL WAYS OF RESPONDING:

- Questions for more information
- Paraphrasing
- Comments
- Compliments

49

Why You Need to Respond Verbally

Conversations have a sequence: a beginning, a middle and an end. The beginning introduces the topic. The middle is where we expand on the topic through listening, asking questions, paraphrasing to check that we understood what the person was saying, making comments or giving compliments. The hard part for children with ADHD/LD is to stay on the topic and try not to change the focus to themselves. Many children need to ask more questions to show their interest.

Asking questions is one of the primary ways we find out if we have anything in common with a new person. It is also a way of showing interest. Asking questions is a way to show we care about someone. We can find out a lot by asking questions. In fact, with people we don't already know, 80% of a conversation consists of asking questions, such as: "How are you doing?" and "Have you been here long?"

> *What happens when you say nothing and don't ask questions?*
>
> *What happens when you just talk about yourself?*
>
> *How does it feel when someone does that to you?*

One of the problems LD/ADHD children have is that they frequently fail to ask other children questions, so the other children don't know they are interested in them.

Also, instead of maintaining the speaker's topic, LD/ADHD children frequently switch topics or start to talk about themselves. Instead of asking questions, they prefer to talk about their own experience that may or may not be related to the topic. The speaker feels as though they don't care about him or her.

> *How do you feel when someone doesn't listen to you?*
>
> *Do you like them?*
>
> *Do you want to spend more time with them? Or*
>
> *Do you go find another friend who shows that he/she cares about you?*

If you only talk about yourself or your experiences and don't ask questions, other children will see you as self-centered, and they avoid you.

Asking Questions

Asking questions is one of the best ways to show someone you are interested in them. By asking questions, we get more information and we let others know whether or not we understand them.

There are two types of questions:

- *closed-ended questions*

- *open-ended questions*

Open-ended questions usually open up the conversation. Open-ended questions ask the speaker to describe the topic in greater detail. Open-ended questions ask the person to tell how he/she feels, thinks or reacts to whatever is being discussed.

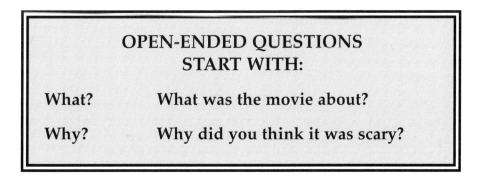

**OPEN-ENDED QUESTIONS
START WITH:**

What?	What was the movie about?
Why?	Why did you think it was scary?

CLOSED-ENDED QUESTIONS

Have a single answer such as Yes or No

Person 1:   What is your name?

Person 2:   John

Person 1:   When did you get here?

Person 2:   Yesterday

Person 1:   (Now what do I say? This guy is real
                  hard to talk to!)

ERRORS IN CONVERSATION

1. Only talking about yourself
2. Failing to listen to the speaker's words or his/her body language
3. Failing to respond to the topic
4. Not showing interest when someone else is talking
5. Interrupting a previous conversation
6. Ignoring nonverbal STOP signs

Starting and Continuing a Conversation

Ask your child:

> *What is the right way to start a conversation?*

Write down your child's answers, then discuss the answers. Discuss the following chart.

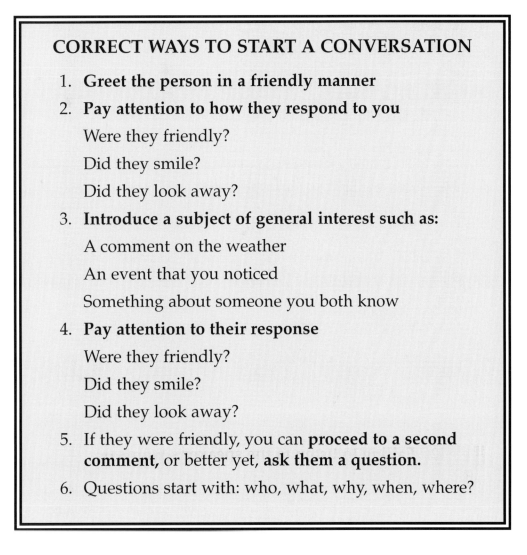

CORRECT WAYS TO START A CONVERSATION

1. **Greet the person in a friendly manner**

2. **Pay attention to how they respond to you**

   Were they friendly?

   Did they smile?

   Did they look away?

3. **Introduce a subject of general interest such as:**

   A comment on the weather

   An event that you noticed

   Something about someone you both know

4. **Pay attention to their response**

   Were they friendly?

   Did they smile?

   Did they look away?

5. If they were friendly, you can **proceed to a second comment,** or better yet, **ask them a question.**

6. Questions start with: who, what, why, when, where?

Other Ways to Continue a Conversation

We have talked about questions, but there are others ways of showing interest. Can you tell me what some of them are?

<u>Statements</u> — give information about content or opinions

<u>Compliments</u> — say what you like, e.g. "Gee, that's cool!" or "lucky" or "I liked the part when you. . . ."

<u>Paraphrasing</u> — repeats what the person has said. It can be a way to ask for more information, e.g. "You said that the sky was green this morning; is that what you meant?"

Paraphrasing questions shows the speaker that you heard the words but aren't sure about the meaning.

Paraphrasing can also be a way to ask for more information.

Review the elements of Active Listening.

ACTIVE LISTENING	
Asking questions	Leads to more information: Who, What, When, How, Why
Encouraging comments	Conveys interest
Clarifying questions	Get more information
Restating	Shows you are listening, understanding, checking
Summarizing	Reviews or pulls ideas together
Validating	Acknowledges the importance of the person or the idea

Play Listening Games with Your Children

There are a number of games that you can play with your children to practice listening.

TV HOST

Practice greeting, making someone feel comfortable, starting and continuing a conversation.

1. One person volunteers to be the TV Host, another person volunteers to be the guest. The role of the TV Host is to greet the guest, to make them feel comfortable, and to get them to talk about something that interests them.

2. Run a timer for two minutes. When the timer goes off, ask your child to make up questions for the speaker. Remind him/her of the question words: WHO? WHAT? WHERE? WHO? HOW? WHEN?

★ Practice asking open-ended questions this week.

Open-ended questions *usually open up the conversation. They ask the person who has been speaking to describe their topic in greater detail.* **Open-ended questions** *ask the person to tell how they feel, think or react to whatever they have been talking about. Open-ended questions start with:*

What?	*What did you think the movie was about?*
Why?	*Why did you think it was scary?*

★ Practice not interrupting this week.

EXERCISE 7: Daily Behavior Chart for Parents

Name: _____

Week of: _____

Directions: Identify the four target behaviors for your child to work on this week and put a check mark each time he/she displays the desired behavior. Be sure to praise your child each time.

Behavior	Mon	Tues	Wed	Thurs	Fri	Sat	Sun
Listening							
Showing Interest							
Asking Questions							
Not Interrupting							

LESSON FOUR:

Nonverbal Conversational Skills

LESSON FOUR: Nonverbal Conversational Skills

The last two lessons have been about conversational skills and the importance of asking questions, making comments or giving compliments. In other words, we not only have to listen, we need to show our interest to the person to whom we are listening. In this lesson, we discuss the importance of eye contact, gestures, body posture, tone, volume and speed.

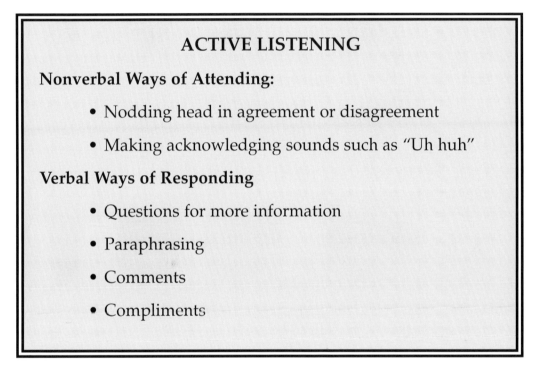

ACTIVE LISTENING

Nonverbal Ways of Attending:

- Nodding head in agreement or disagreement

- Making acknowledging sounds such as "Uh huh"

Verbal Ways of Responding

- Questions for more information

- Paraphrasing

- Comments

- Compliments

We are going to practice judging people better by learning to read their nonverbal body language.

Gestures, Tone, Personal Space

In the last lesson, we talked about how to use questions and comments in a conversation. We also let people know how we feel without using words. This nonverbal expression is known as body language. In this lesson we are going to talk about how to judge people better by learning to read their nonverbal body language.

Nonverbal signals are 60% of any communication. People use their bodies to communicate feelings, interest, or lack of interest. They use tone to express anger, annoyance, or happiness. One of the most effective ways to understanding what a person means is to understand their body language. Many children are so intent on understanding the words, that they don't pay attention to the emotional message in the tone or body language. Since this is a weakness in many children with Learning Disabilities, parents need to spend more time on this section to ensure their child can track the emotional message of body language.

We have talked about three aspects of nonverbal communication:

1. The importance of gestures and facial expressions

2. The importance of tone and volume

3. The importance of respecting personal space

We know a little about body language.

Can you tell me what you have learned so far?

If your child does not answer, point to your eyes.

What do the eyes tell us about a person?

> **Answer:** *A person's eyes tell us how they feel . . .*

Demonstrate the Importance of Facial Expressions

A person's tone, gesture or facial expression tell you what the person is really feeling. Understanding how to read facial expressions can help your child understand people better.

When the Nonverbal and the Verbal Message Disagree

Demonstrate saying something to your child, while purposely trying to send a contradictory message with your tone or facial expressions. While using an exaggerated, angry tone, tight mouth, tight, squinting eyes and fists clenched, say:

"I'm really happy today."

Ask your child:

Did you believe that I was happy?

Your child should say "no." Ask your child,

Why didn't you believe me?

Write down what your child says, reminding him/her to be specific:

1. You looked cross

2. Your eyes looked down

3. Your mouth was clenched

4. Your tone sounded angry

What about my tone?

Was it friendly or unfriendly?

Did it sound happy or angry?

Was my body posture friendly or unfriendly?

When you ask, use a friendly tone and open body posture. Then demonstrate unfriendly tone and closed body posture.

My body language told you how I was feeling.

What are some of the reasons you need to know how someone feels?

1. To respond to them correctly

2. To judge interest

3. To understand what they are saying

4. To judge if this is a good time to approach them

5. To understand jokes

If the words and the body language disagree, which one is more likely to tell you the person's true feelings?

Answer: *Body Language*

People often say what they think you would like to hear, but their body language *seldom* lies. Gestures, facial expressions and tone are more accurate indicators of a person's feelings. Many children with LD/ADHD listen to the words but ignore the body language.

It is important that children understand that **body language always tells how a person feels**. Children may not know what caused the feeling, so it is important to check if the feeling is about something that they may have said or done.

Read the emotion in the body language.

Check to see if you said or did something that upset the other person.

What are the Components of Body Language?

How do we communicate with our bodies? Can you give some examples?

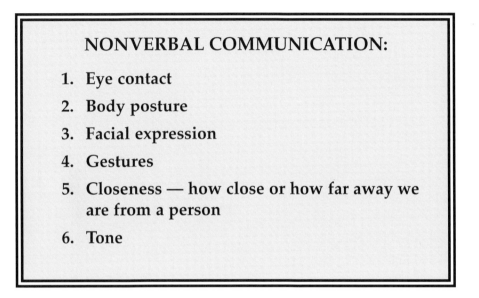

NONVERBAL COMMUNICATION:

1. **Eye contact**
2. **Body posture**
3. **Facial expression**
4. **Gestures**
5. **Closeness — how close or how far away we are from a person**
6. **Tone**

Gestures, tone and posture tell us what people feel. Their posture can show if they are interested or not. You can learn a lot about people by watching their gestures, their facial expressions and by listening to their tone.

Practice Reading Body Language

One of the easiest ways to practice reading body language is to watch a sitcom on television with the sound turned off. While you watch the show, ask your child to tell you what is going on between the actors. Since actors frequently exaggerate the emotional message, they are often fairly easy to read.

Ask your child:

1. What do the eyes say?

2. What about the facial expressions? Is the person happy, sad, angry?

3. Make up a story about the people in the sitcom on T.V.

At various times during the week, ask your child to identify how you are feeling by reading your body language. Are you in a hurry, harried, happy, glad, relaxed, open, uptight?

Make it a game to act out feelings. Collect pictures of people or purchase cards that have pictures of children expressing different feelings. Another activity is that you can make cards of people who express the following feelings:

Fearful	Lucky	Anxious	Relieved
Angry	Embarrassed	Frustrated	Overwhelmed
Sad	Important	Bored	Guilty
Jealous	Proud	Happy	Disgusted

The Importance of Tone

The tone of voice we use, whether angry, annoyed or happy, tells other people how we feel. People react to our tone more than they do to our words, so we need to make sure that our tone communicates what we want it to communicate.

Illustrate using an angry tone while saying:

". . . gee, that sounds real interesting."

Ask your child for feedback.

Did you believe that I thought it was interesting?

Did you pay more attention to my tone or my words?

Tone can be cheerful, angry, teasing, bored, mean, sincere, or friendly.

If your tone contradicts the verbal message, people pay more attention to the tone than the words. People hear the words, but they react to the tone.

Disagreements between the Words and the Tone

What if the words and the tone disagree?

Provide an example of when the words and the tone disagree.

Adopt an angry, mean look and say:

"I love you."

Ask your child for feedback.

Did you think I meant it? Why didn't you believe me?

Did you pay more attention to my words or to my tone?

Remember people's body language is more reliable than their words. One of the most common mistakes is to ignore the importance of the tone, posture, facial gestures and the use of space. If the words and tone disagree, pay more attention to the tone because it more accurately reflects what the speaker is feeling.

Jokes

Jokes are often funny because the words and the nonverbal body language disagree. Children with Learning Disabilities frequently miss jokes because they pay attention to the words and ignore or misunderstand the tone. If one says something serious with a silly expression on their face, the facial expression tells us that the message is supposed to be funny.

DEMONSTRATION:

Have your child pretend to finish an ice cream cone and complain he/she didn't like it.

You respond by saying, "I see how much you didn't like it," using an affectionate, teasing tone.

When the tone contradicts the words, the child has to determine if the tone is friendly.

When someone teases you in a friendly way, it is meant to be funny.

LD/ADHD children frequently misunderstand jokes because they believe the words and forget to pay attention to the tone. They also have trouble separating friendly teasing from unfriendly teasing because they don't pay enough attention to tone and body language.

> **QUESTIONS FOR THE CHILD TO ASK:**
>
> * *Is the tone serious?*
> * *Is the person teasing me in a playful way?*
> * *Is the person using a friendly tone?*

Understanding jokes requires the ability to do more than one thing at a time. Children need to hear the words, interpret the tone or body language, and then figure out if they agree or disagree. Lastly, when children do not get a joke, they don't have to announce to the group that they didn't get it. They can just laugh along with the other children. Afterwards, they can ask their parents or a close friend to explain it to them.

> Teach your child to laugh when everyone else is laughing. He/she does not need to announce that he/she hasn't understood what is funny.

Sarcasm

Sarcasm is harder for ADHD/LD children to grasp. The person using sarcasm often expects that we will know that they are not being serious and so we are supposed to disregard the negative comment. In some cases, they expect that we will find the comment funny because of the exaggeration. Most people telling a joke will give it away by having a twinkle in their eyes or a smirk around their mouths. In contrast, the person who uses sarcasm often looks very serious and so LD children often believe people who use exaggeration really believe what they are saying is true.

Personal Space, Distance, and Touching

Have you ever had the experience of someone who you didn't know very well getting too close to you?

> *What did you do?*

> *Did you back up?*

> *Did you feel uncomfortable?*

Everyone has a space around them that they feel is their personal space. This is called "personal space" and is different in various countries and cultures. Here in the United States, people generally prefer their personal space to be an arm's length or approximately 2.5–3 feet.

Demonstrate by putting out your arm:

If you were to draw a circle around yourself, holding your arm out, this would define your personal space.

You may let a close friend enter your personal space, but if someone is not very special to you, you may not like that person being too close.

It is a mistake to get too close to someone that you don't know very well; that person may feel you are invading his/her "personal space."

How do you feel when someone that you don't know well gets really close to you? Do you like it? Do you want to pull away?

Most people do not like feeling invaded so it is very important to learn not to get too close to someone whom you don't know well.

*Pay attention if you get too close. Does the person pull away? If he/she does, that is a **STOP** Sign.*

Practice using:

- appropriate tone

- appropriate distance

- "interested" facial gestures

BODY LANGUAGE MISTAKES

1. Violating a person's personal space
2. Using too loud or harsh a tone when you speak
3. Failing to make eye contact
4. Failing to monitor facial expressions that show disapproval or lack of interest
5. Failing to stop when someone asks you to STOP

Review the Most Common Body Language Mistakes

1. Reading the tone or body language incorrectly

2. Disregarding an annoyed, angry or irritated tone

3. Disregarding a bored expression

4. Getting into someone's space by touching him/her or taking something

Remember, if we watch the other person and listen to their bodies, we can figure out what the other person might be feeling by noticing:

1. *Expressions in eyes*

2. *Eye contact or lack of eye contact*

3. *Body posture (open or closed)*

4. *Facial expressions*

5. *How the person stands*

6. *Proximity, the use of distance or closeness, is an expression comfort or discomfort*

7. *Gestures*

★ *Pay attention this week to some of these messages such as facial*

69

expression, body posture or tone. See if you can read if the person is interested or bored. If uninterested, should you:

1. *Ignore the person and keep telling your story?*

2. *Change the subject?*

3. *Ask if he/she is listening? Or,*

4. *Ask them a question about him/herself?*

★ *Pay attention to nonverbal messages by watching:*

- *Facial expression*

- *Body posture*

- *Tone*

EXERCISE 8: Volume Control

Look at these pictures. Think about the importance of volume.

Have you ever been around a boy or girl who talked too loudly?

Did you want to tell them to be quiet?

Has anyone ever told you that you talk too loudly or too softly?

Using the right volume is important.

There are times when it's okay to be loud, as when you are rooting for your team at a baseball game, or when you are applauding at a concert.

There are also times when you need to speak softly and use less volume.

When would you want to use a softer voice?

Circle which times you would want to use a soft voice:

At the library

At the movie theater

When you answer your teacher

When you tell someone a secret

★ Ask your parents if you ever speak too quietly or too loudly.

EXERCISE 9: The Right Tone of Voice

The tone of voice that we use, whether it is an angry, annoyed or happy tone, tells other people how we feel. People react to our tone more than they react to our words, so make sure that your tone communicates what you want it to do. Ask for feedback on your tone.

Look over these situations and then,
circle what kind of tone you should use.

Your mother tells you a friend is on the telephone. You take the phone and say "hi." Your tone is:

cheerful   angry   teasing   bored   mean   sincere

Your teacher asks you to sit down and get back to your school work. You answer, " O.K." Try saying "O.K." in a **snotty** tone.

How will the teacher respond to you? _____

A friend tells you that you are cute. Try saying "thanks" with a **friendly** tone. Now use a **bored** tone.

Which one will get you more compliments in the future?

Your dad reminds you to take out the garbage. His tone is annoyed. You should answer him in

❑   a **sarcastic** tone?   ❑   a **sincere** tone?

How will your dad respond if you answer him in an **angry** tone?

★   Practice using a **friendly tone** this week.

EXERCISE 10: Facial Expressions

Facial expressions can tell you how someone is feeling.

Connect the feelings with the pictures.

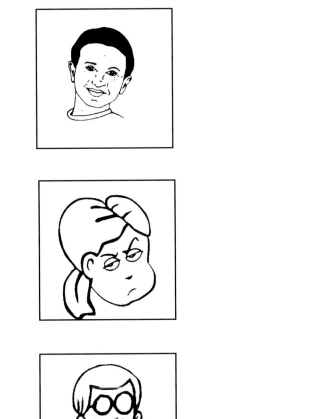

I'M HAPPY

I FEEL O.K.

I DON'T GET IT

I'M ANGRY

EXERCISE 11: Body Language

DIRECTIONS: For each picture below describe:

Feeling: _____   Feeling: _____

Body part(s) _____   Body part(s) _____

Feeling: _____   Feeling: _____

Body part(s) _____   Body part(s) _____

EXERCISE 12: Physical Proximity

When you get too close to people, they feel uncomfortable. Every culture has a different notion of what feels too close.

What do you think too close is in our culture?

Answer: *About an arm's length away.*

What is wrong in this picture?

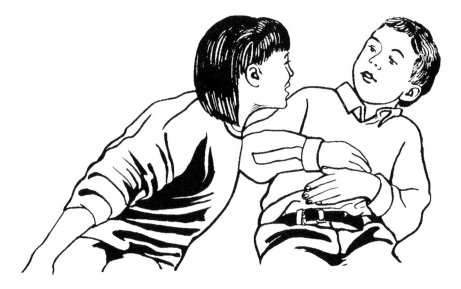

Draw a picture so both children are comfortable. How far away from each other would they be?

LESSON FIVE:

Recognizing Friendly Behavior

LESSON FIVE: Recognizing Friendly Behavior

During the last lesson, we showed nonverbal ways people communicate with each other. We also learned that "body language" is sometimes more honest and reliable than the verbal messages.

If there is a conflict between the verbal and nonverbal message, which one should you believe?

Answer: *The nonverbal message*

How do people express themselves nonverbally?

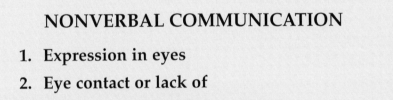

NONVERBAL COMMUNICATION

1. **Expression in eyes**
2. **Eye contact or lack of**
3. **Open or closed body posture**
4. **Facial expression**
5. **The distance the person stands (proximity)**
6. **Gestures**

Now, let's talk about recognizing and obeying verbal and nonverbal **STOP** *signs.*

STOP Signs

*People tell us through their body language how they feel. Our goal is to know from observing the body language if people are feeling friendly towards us (approachable signs), or if they want to be left alone. We want to practice interpreting friendly behavior and paying attention to nonverbal **STOP** signs.*

*Why is it important to know the **STOP** signs that people use?*

- *To judge if it is a good time to approach them*

- *To understand how they feel*

- *To respect others' needs and wants*

*If you recognize **STOP** signs, you will know more about approaching people, how to join groups, and how to show respect for others.*

When you don't pay attention or respect what someone else wants, do they:

    1. Want to be closer to you (be your friend)? or

    2. Want to avoid you?

People React to Your Behavior

Your behavior makes people want to:

- **Approach you or**

- **Avoid you**

What are the most common mistakes made by children with ADHD and Learning Disabilities?

1. Failure to read the tone or body language

2. Disregarding an annoyed tone

3. Disregarding a bored expression

4. Failure to stop talking when they see **STOP** signs

DEMONSTRATE STOP SIGNS

I'm on the telephone, talking to your father. You come in and start talking to me.

Look at my body language.

What does it tell you?

Demonstrate an annoyed or angry expression

Let's describe what you saw.

Review:

My eyes got smaller. I didn't smile.

My body stiffened. I may have frowned.

Did my body language say, "come here" or "go away?"

Answer: *Go away.*

What happens when you don't wait?

Answer: *The person gets angry.*

Review this chart and discuss the elements of body language.

NONVERBAL COMMUNICATION

1. Expression in eyes: friendly or unfriendly?

2. Eye contact or lack of eye contact

3. Body posture: open or closed?

4. Facial expression: happy, sad, angry, annoyed, or frightened?

5. Posture and gestures: open or closed?

6. Distance: does the person stand close or far away?

7. Inclination: does he/she lean away or towards you?

8. Tone: does he/she sound annoyed or angry?

Discuss nonverbal **STOP** signs.

STOP SIGNS

1. Person looks away repeatedly

2. Person turns away

3. Person crosses arms and looks unfriendly

4. Person starts to back away from you

5. Person's facial expression looks bored

6. Person speaks in an annoyed/or bored tone

When you ignore unfriendly body language or facial cues, people get upset with you.

Here is a checklist to use when you watch people. If you want to tell people something special, you need to consider, "Is this a good time to approach them?" Go through the nonverbal checklist to see if you can tell the answer.

1. Is the **expression** in their eyes friendly or unfriendly?

2. Is there **eye contact** or lack of eye contact?

3. Is their **body posture** open or closed?

4. Is their **facial expression** happy, sad, angry, annoyed or frightened?

5. Are their **posture or gestures** open or closed?

6. Do they **stand close or far away**?

7. Do people **lean towards or away from you**?

If people send out **STOP** signs should you:

1. Ignore them and keep telling your story?

2. Change the subject?

3. Ask them a question about themselves? Or

4. Ask them if they are listening?

Play Red Light/Green Light

Hand out pictures or cards with different feelings pictured on them to your child. Ask your child to describe what he/she sees: is the person *friendly* or *unfriendly*? Ask your child to act out the emotional state that the card indicates. If the face is friendly, it means you have a **green** light. If the face is unfriendly or indifferent, it is a **red** light. Use cards to act out the following feelings:

FEAR

ANGER

SADNESS

ANXIETY

HAPPINESS

Which feelings say approach?

Which feelings might be ***STOP*** *signs?*

With younger children, you can make or purchase a red octagonal **STOP** sign. One side can have a green light and the other side can say **STOP**. Act out these four situations and ask your child to identify your feeling and whether your nonverbal communication says to "come closer" or "stop and wait."

Happy:	Relaxed muscles, easy smile, laughing
Angry:	Tight muscles, no smile, glaring
Anxious:	Tight muscles, avoid eye contact
Friendly:	Relaxed muscles, easy smile, eye contact

Which feelings say ***APPROACH****?*

Which feelings might say ***STOP****?*

Reading STOP Signs

We have been talking about paying attention to how people tell us nonverbally if they want us to come closer or to stay away.

*We have called these nonverbal "stay away" signals **STOP** signs.*

*We have also been discussing the importance of respecting other people and their desires. We have talked about what happens when you approach someone who wants to be left alone. Why is it important to know the **STOP** signs?*

Why is it important to pay attention to what other people want?

How do you feel when someone ignores what you want?

Answers: *It makes you angry.*

It makes you sad.

If you don't pay attention or respect what others want, they want to avoid you.

Ignoring STOP signs causes people to avoid you

EXERCISE 13: Reading Body Language

When people feel friendly towards you, they show you with their body language and facial gestures.

Circle the children who look unfriendly.

EXERCISE 14: STOP Signs

When people don't want to talk to us, they also give us signs.

We call these **STOP signs**.

- Looking away repeatedly

- Turning away

- Crossing arms and looking away

- Backing away from you

- Lacking enthusiasm

PAY ATTENTION TO STOP SIGNS

Circle answers that will make both of you feel more comfortable

When you see **STOP** signs should you:

- Ignore the **STOP** signs?

- Change the subject?

- Ask a question? or

- Ask if they are listening to you?

LESSON SIX:

Joining an Ongoing Group

LESSON SIX: Joining an Ongoing Group

We have looked at the nonverbal ways people use to communicate and have identified friendly versus unfriendly behaviors. People show interest in us nonverbally by:

1. *Making eye contact*

2. *Smiling*

3. *Extending greetings*

4. *Friendly gestures*

5. *Friendly facial expressions*

*The **STOP** signs include:*

1. *Avoiding eye contact*

2. *Frowning instead of smiling*

3. *Failing to acknowledge your presence, e.g. no verbal or nonverbal greeting*

*Why is it important to know the **STOP** signs people use?*

1. *To judge if it is a good time to approach someone*

2. *To understand how others are feeling*

3. *To respect other people and their needs and wants*

*If you recognize **STOP** signs, you will know how to approach people, join groups and show respect for others.*

Joining a Group

Learning how to join an ongoing activity is a skill. We are going to use our new knowledge of judging whether we are given a green or a red light to determine when to approach a group. In other words, only approach a group if the children are being friendly. Judge this by reading their body language.

Why do you think we need to know how to join a group?

How do we judge whether children are being friendly or unfriendly?

Emphasize the following points to your child:

1. Protect yourself from getting hurt.

2. Respect what other people want.

Join, Don't Intrude

Offer the following scenario.

> ## SCENARIO:
>
> *You want to join an ongoing volleyball game or basketball game.*
>
> *You notice that there are a group of children playing, and they seem to be short one person.*
>
> *How do you join the game?*

Most ADHD/LD children go right up and ask if they can play. If the children aren't ready to include someone else, they will say no. If your child can judge interest, they can protect themselves from feeling rejected. When psychologists studied how popular children join activities, they found that popular children do it differently than many ADHD/LD children.

What do popular children do?

Answers:

- *They wait.*

- *They watch.*

- *They join as an observer and make friendly comments.*

- *They give compliments.*

- *They wait to be invited to join.*

- *If they aren't invited, they either continue to watch or go elsewhere to play.*

How do unpopular children try to join?

- *They barge in.*

- *They brag about how well they can play.*

- *They tease or put-down the other children if they aren't invited to play with them.*

Many LD/ADHD children initiate contact with other children with disruptive, or self-centered behaviors, e.g. "I know how to play that," or "That's a stupid game."

Demonstrate How to Join a Group the Wrong Way

You need a minimum of three people to demonstrate this activity. Two of the participants pretend to play a game, such as an imaginary card game (using a deck of cards). One of the parents plays a newcomer and tries to join by:

1. Bragging that he/she can play better

2. Grabbing the cards

3. Making fun of the game

93

Discuss how it felt when the newcomer intruded on the activity.

1. What was wrong with how the outsider joined?

2. How did it feel to have your play interrupted?

Now demonstrate approaching the group the correct way. Here are the elements that need to be in your role-play:

1. <u>Approach</u> gradually within two to three feet.

2. <u>Greet</u> the participants.

3. <u>Wait</u> and watch what they are doing for at least one minute.

4. <u>Make a comment</u> about the game. If possible, give a compliment to the participants.

5. <u>OBSERVE</u> how they respond to you. If they aren't demonstrating friendly body language, *do not ask if you can play*.

6. <u>WAIT</u> until a member of the group gives you a ***green*** light.

After role-playing the correct way, ask if they can identify what you did. Write down their answers.

Go over the answers, making sure that they understand conceptually what they need to do. Reverse roles.

Reiterate How to Join a Group

Successful children approach gradually. They approach a group and observe the game. As they watch, they collect information about the other children and their activities. They observe the other children's body language. If children are unfriendly, they don't ask to join the activity.

Ask your child to describe how to join a group the correct way.

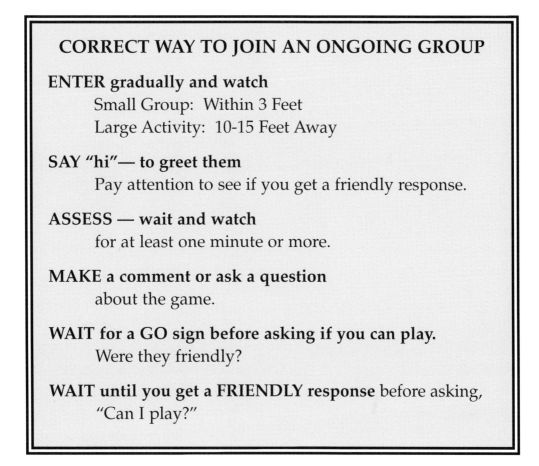

CORRECT WAY TO JOIN AN ONGOING GROUP

ENTER gradually and watch
Small Group: Within 3 Feet
Large Activity: 10-15 Feet Away

SAY "hi"— to greet them
Pay attention to see if you get a friendly response.

ASSESS — wait and watch
for at least one minute or more.

MAKE a comment or ask a question
about the game.

WAIT for a GO sign before asking if you can play.
Were they friendly?

WAIT until you get a FRIENDLY response before asking,
"Can I play?"

Successful children express interest in social contact. Children need to greet the children and engage in other-directed questions, comments or compliments:

"That was a good throw!"

"That looks like fun."

"You're good at this."

Or with a question such as, *"What's the score?"*

Popular children show their interest but do not push themselves on other children. They look for an opening and either wait to be invited, or ask gently if they can play if the children seem friendly. If not, they wait and watch or find another activity.

Coach your child on:

1. Proximity

2. Eye contact

3. Waiting and making positive comments

4. Respecting nonverbal STOP signs

Inclusion or Exclusion?

*Do other children **have** to include you?*

Some children feel that they have a right to be included. The truth is that children have the right to exclude other children, even if the rules at school say that they *have* to include everyone. Children can and do find ways to exclude someone whom they don't like, or whom they think is pushy, etc.

How do you handle it if the children say you can't join their game?

This is a hard topic. Many children feel rejection keenly; they want to lash out at the children for hurting them. Parents need to discuss the difference between refusal versus rejection with their children.

What is the difference between refusal and rejection?

Popular children perceive rejection as a refusal, e.g. "This isn't a good time for you to join our group" instead of *"We don't like you."*

Children who have problems with social skills usually interpret a refusal as a personal rejection. They assume that other children don't want to play with them at all. In some instances, this is true because the other children don't like their bossy behavior. Instead of respecting other children and their right to have private time together, LD/ADHD children tend to push themselves on children. This pushiness makes other children want to avoid them even more. It becomes a vicious circle of rejection.

Encourage children to talk about being refused. It is not necessary to do anything other than acknowledge that they probably have had their feelings hurt and that they need to seek out other children who like them.

If children mention that they play sports poorly and other children don't want them on their team, ask if there is something else they can do while the other children play. The important point to communicate is that we all have strengths and weaknesses, and we need to learn to look to our strengths and accept our weaknesses. If children have trouble with this concept, ask:

> *Have you ever excluded anyone?*

> *Why did you do it?*

Conclude this section with a summary of the differences between **refusal vs. rejection**.

> *When someone refuses you, it is because:*

> *1. It isn't a good time for them.*

> *2. They may be involved in a game and do not want to start over.*

> *3. They don't want to include a new person.*

Offer the following principle:

> *Children have a right to refuse you. But if they do, it doesn't mean you're not O.K. Focus on the people who like you.*

> *Have your child observe popular children and how they join a group. Discuss it.*

> *1. They waited.*

> *2. They weren't too pushy.*

> *3. They didn't mind if we said "no."*

> *4. They respected our game and our rules.*

EXERCISE 15: Practice Joining an Ongoing Group

1. **STEP ONE: Enter** on the sidelines and watch.

2. **STEP TWO: Say** something friendly.

3. **STEP THREE: Assess** the children by reading their body language.
   Are they friendly?
   Do they look at you and smile?
   Do they acknowledge you or are they ignoring you?

4. **STEP FOUR: Give** compliments or ask questions.

5. **STEP FIVE: Wait** for a YES signal, e.g. they ask you to join them or respond to you in a friendly way.

6. **STEP SIX:** If they aren't friendly, **find** another activity.

Following this review, initiate a discussion that elaborates the theme of joining an ongoing activity.

Do other children have to include you?

HOW DO YOU HANDLE IT IF CHILDREN SAY YOU CAN'T JOIN THEIR GAME?

Wrong: Tell them you don't want to play their stupid game!

Right: Find someone else who wants to play with you.

★ **Respect** other people and their desires to be alone or with someone else.

LESSON SEVEN:

Dealing with Teasing

LESSON SEVEN: Dealing with Teasing

*In the last lesson, we talked about strategies to join an ongoing group. If you ignore **STOP** signs, sometimes children tease you. Let's review the steps to joining an ongoing group while paying attention to the **STOP** signs.*

HOW DO YOU JOIN AN ONGOING GROUP?

1. **Approach gradually**
2. **Greet the children**
3. **Pay attention to their body language**
4. **Observe them and ask a question or make a comment**
5. **Wait to see if they display friendly behavior**
6. **If they don't seem friendly, either watch, or go play with someone else**

Pay attention to STOP signs. If the children give you unfriendly signs, do not approach them and ask to play. Unfriendly signs include:

1. *Avoiding eye contact*

2. *Not smiling*

3. *Not acknowledging your presence*

What happens if you force yourself on people who don't want to be with you?

1. *They get annoyed.*

2. *They put you down.*

3. *They may get aggressive.*

4. *They may tease you.*

5. *They may want to avoid you in the future.*

Teasing

How do most children handle teasing?

Answer: They get upset. They try to tease the other child back. Sometimes, they get aggressive and attack.

Does hurting another child ever get them to stop teasing you?

Answer: Not usually.

Why You Need to Know How to Handle Teasing

Teasing is the hardest things for children to handle well.

Why do you think other children tease?

- To feel better about themselves

- To deal with jealous feelings

- To feel superior

- To make you feel bad

Usually children who tease others don't feel very good about themselves. They are usually either jealous or insecure.

Do children who feel secure about themselves tease others? Why does teasing bother us?

Answer: It hurts our feelings because we feel insecure about ourselves.

What happens if a friend teases you about something that you like or have accepted about yourself?

Answer: Most of the time, we don't get upset. We recognize the difference between friendly joking teasing and unfriendly teasing.

Many LD/ADHD children can't distinguish between friendly and unfriendly teasing. They don't distinguish the other child's intentions.

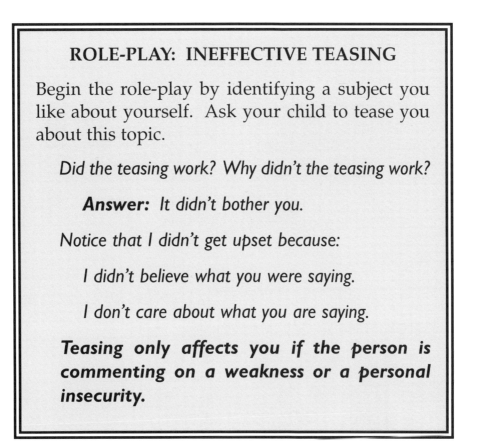

ROLE-PLAY: INEFFECTIVE TEASING

Begin the role-play by identifying a subject you like about yourself. Ask your child to tease you about this topic.

Did the teasing work? Why didn't the teasing work?

Answer: *It didn't bother you.*

Notice that I didn't get upset because:

I didn't believe what you were saying.

I don't care about what you are saying.

Teasing only affects you if the person is commenting on a weakness or a personal insecurity.

The Wrong Way to Handle Teasing

The goal of teasing is to see if you will get upset.

Ask your child to tease you about your shirt.

You can demonstrate handling teasing the wrong way by:

1. Getting angry

2. Calling names

3. Teasing back

4. Hitting (act it out)

WRONG WAY TO HANDLE TEASING:

- **Name-calling**
- **Telling the teacher (for older children)**
- **Hitting**
- **Crying**
- **Withdrawing**
- **Getting angry**

Can you tell me why these don't work very well?

Your child guesses:

- The other children get angry.

- Children want to hurt you too.

- Children tell other children.

What is the goal of teasing?

> **Answer:** *To get you upset*

Three Strategies to Handle Teasing

*The only way to win with teasing is to show the children who are teasing you that what they say **doesn't matter to you**.*

There are three ways you can respond to teasing:

*1. **Ignore the words***

Show me how to ignore someone:

- *You say nothing in response.*

- *You don't look at the child.*

- *You keep doing what you are doing.*

- *You ask a redirecting question about a totally different topic as though you had not heard the jibe.*

2. **Agree with the words**

   Show me how to agree with me:

   - *"Boy, does your hair look silly."*

   - *"Yes, it didn't do what I wanted it to do today."*

3. **Agree by making a joke out of the teasing.**

   "You mean my new 50's look [laughing]. Don't you think I look smart?"

   What message does a child get if you:

   - *Ignore them*

   - *Agree with them, or*

   - *Make a joke out of their teasing?*

   Answer: *They see it doesn't matter to you, and you aren't going to get upset.*

   Does the child who reacts get teased more?

   Answer: *Yes.*

Role-play Being Teased

The most effective way to learn how to handle teasing is to allow yourself to be teased in a safe setting. Start off by volunteering to be teased first. The first step is to establish "safe" boundaries; you define what YOU CAN AND CANNOT be teased about. It is important to establish boundaries. You begin by asking your child to say one teasing comment to you. You model handling the comment by using **one** of these three methods:

1. Ignoring the comment

2. Agreeing with the comment or

3. Making a joke of the comment

Ask your child to go next. Make sure he/she understands the idea is to not react to teasing. Have your child set boundaries by defining what is safe and what is off-limits. It is very helpful if the child is willing to share the quality or characteristic to which he/she reacts when teased. Start with a safe topic. When your child has mastered one of these methods, ask if it is okay to be teased about a sensitive topic. Only proceed if your child is willing. If your child feels that this subject is too painful, you make the topic **out-of-bounds**. (Example: child with a Learning Disability doesn't want to be teased about being a poor speller.)

This is a good time to remind your child that we all have good qualities and we all have weaknesses; it takes a strong person to admit one's own weaknesses. In this role-play, you play a particularly active role both modeling the appropriate responses and coaching.

Review:

> *The purpose of teasing is to get a reaction out of you.*
>
> *Why do kids tease?*
>
>> ***Answer:*** *Because they don't feel good about themselves.*

THREE WAYS TO HANDLE TEASING:

> *1. Ignore the words by asking a redirecting question.*
>
> *2. Agree with the comment.*
>
> *3. Agree with the comment and make a joke out of it.*

★ Practice handling teasing

LESSON EIGHT:

Managing Anger

LESSON EIGHT: Managing Anger

Note to parents: Some children need an extra lesson on teasing and/ or joining an ongoing group. If this is the case, the parent should repeat the given lesson in place of going on to this one.

We have talked about how to deal with teasing. Teasing hurts our feelings and makes us angry. What is the goal of teasing you?

> **Answer:** *To get you upset*

We said that there are three major ways to deal with teasing. Do you remember them?

> *1. Ignore the words (walk away or ask a redirecting question).*
>
> *2. Agree with the teaser.*
>
> *3. Agree by making a joke out of the teasing.*

The only way to win with teasing is to act as if it doesn't bother you!

Teasing is one of the ways our feelings get hurt. There are other ways we get hurt. Some of us get angry when we get hurt. We are going to talk about handling anger better.

Anger is a difficult emotion to control because we are usually hurt when we are angry. What are some of the things that hurt our feelings and make us angry?

> • *Jealousy*
>
> • *Fear*
>
> • *Embarrassment*
>
> • *Hurt*

While we can't control the things that make us angry, we ***can*** *control how we act.*

How to Handle Anger Better

Why is it important to control what you do when you get angry? While you might want to strike back, either verbally or physically, you need to think about your choices. Many people do or say things when they are angry that they later regret.

Give me an example of something you did when you were angry that you regretted later?

- *Hurt someone*

- *Called them a name*

- *Took something of theirs*

- *Broke something*

- *Hurt yourself*

Why do you think you might regret some angry actions?

Answers:

- *You lose friends*

- *People withdraw from you*

- *You break something you care about*

- *You hurt someone and they won't forgive you*

- *You hurt yourself*

Two Ways to Deal with Anger

There are two really good ways to deal with anger:

1. *Talk about it.*

2. *Ignore it and walk away.*

For example, some children say something mean to you. You don't know them and you probably won't see them again. What are your choices:

- *You can call them a name back.*

- *You can ask them, "What's your problem?"*

- *You can say nothing, walk away and think to yourself, "I wonder what's bothering them today?"*

Recognizing Physical Responses to Anger

Most people have a very physical response to anger. For many ADHD children the response happens very quickly. Blood flows into the brainstem, the heartbeat increases, and blood flow increases to large muscle groups in the legs and arms. An angry person is more mentally alert, and his/her body is ready to fight or to flee. This physical response is different from feeling sad, jealous, glad, or happy. Unfortunately, many ADHD people like the alert feeling which anger brings.

Our bodies react physically to anger and for some of us, this process happens very quickly. For many of us the cooling out period may take 20 to 25 minutes or even a few hours.

There are different styles of handling angry feelings:

Shark:	*Is aggressive and attacks*
Teddy bear:	*Apologizes, gives you a hug*
Turtle:	*Goes away and avoids*
Owl:	*Tries to talk it out*

How do you get angry?

What style do you use to express your anger?

Do you know how long your cooling off period is?

PRINCIPLES

1. We cannot always control what we feel.
2. We CAN control what we DO with our feelings.
3. Our actions affect others.
4. People react to anger with anger or they avoid the person who's angry.
5. We need to think before choosing an action because people who are angry create reactions in others.

Handling Anger the Wrong Way

Act out the following situation:

You are playing with a toy and some children come and take it from you. What do you do?

Discuss the wrong way of handling it:

- *You call them a name.*

- *You hit them.*

- *You grab the toy back.*

Discuss the consequences of the actions.

What would be a better solution?

- *Ask for the toy back.*

- *Get an adult to help you get it back.*

- *Tell the children you won't play with them if they play this way.*

Have a discussion about how it felt during this role-play.

Processing Anger

Here are seven steps to use when dealing with anger.

1. **Identify feelings:** *Think: what am I feeling? Am I jealous? Scared? Hurt?*

2. **Reflect:** *Did the person intend to hurt me?*

3. **Consider:** *If the person intended to hurt you, ask yourself, did I hurt him/her first?*

4. **Question:** *Do I need to apologize? Most of the time, people hurt others without intending to do so. Many times, apologizing helps resolve the conflict.*

5. **Think:** *What are my choices? Fight back? Retreat? Apologize? Think about it?*

6. **Take a break:** *Sometimes when you're really worked up, you may need to step back from the situation by leaving the room or the house. Sometimes doing something physical like taking a walk, running, or hitting a punching bag, helps your body calm down so that you can carefully consider your choices.*

7. **Choose your best option:** *remember that there will be consequences to your actions.*

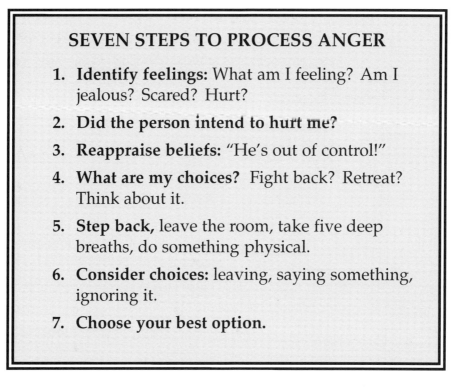

SEVEN STEPS TO PROCESS ANGER

1. **Identify feelings:** What am I feeling? Am I jealous? Scared? Hurt?

2. **Did the person intend to hurt me?**

3. **Reappraise beliefs:** "He's out of control!"

4. **What are my choices?** Fight back? Retreat? Think about it.

5. **Step back,** leave the room, take five deep breaths, do something physical.

6. **Consider choices:** leaving, saying something, ignoring it.

7. **Choose your best option.**

Role-play Handling Anger

Re-enact the same situation as above, except do it the right way.

You are playing with a toy and someone comes and takes it from you. What do you do?

- *Identify feelings: Think: what you are feeling? Am you jealous? Scared? Hurt?* **I'm angry.**

- *Reflect: Did the person intend to hurt you?* **Maybe not.**

- *Consider: Did the person intend to hurt you? Ask yourself, did I hurt him/her first?* **You might be unaware of something you said or did to hurt the other person.**

- *Question: Do you need to apologize? Most of the time, people hurt others without intending to do so. Many times, apologizing for your part helps resolve the conflict.*

- *Think:* What are my choices? Fight back? Retreat? Apologize? Think about it? Ask for it back? Ask an adult for help? Bargain with the child? Go find something else to do?

- *Take a break:* If you're really worked up, step back from the situation by leaving the room or the house.

- *Choose your best option.* Remember that there will be consequences to your actions.

Many children with ADHD find it hard to handle anger well; they may even find it exciting. Anger stimulates their brain and makes them feel more alert. When hurt, some children who have impulse problems cannot control their desire to react. They may react so quickly that there isn't time to engage in any of these steps. Many children can be helped by medication.

Rehearse Handling Anger Differently

When you are so angry you feel you need to do something, use one of these safe ways to deal with anger.

SAFE WAYS TO DEAL WITH ANGER

1. **Vent:** Hit a pillow, go for a run, throw a basketball, hit a punching bag, yell at an imaginary version of the person.

2. **Sidestep power struggles:** If you see someone is agitated, do not bring up a conflict. Change the subject.

3. **Take a break and do something physical.** Take a walk or run.

4. **Discover the hurt behind the anger.** Examine your feelings. Acknowledge the hurt you caused others.

5. **Turn anger into action.** What can you do with the anger to change the situation?

6. **Reframe the message.** Step outside of yourself. Try to see the trigger to your anger as something that isn't really about you, e.g. your dad comes home in a bad mood and yells at you. Don't take it personally, he may have had a bad day.

★ *Think about things that make you angry. Use SAFE WAYS to deal with anger this week.*

Apologizing

Apologizing is an important skill. Everyone makes mistakes, and hurts others. We need to know how to say, "I'm sorry." Sometimes, the best way to handle an angry person is to apologize for making the person feel badly.

★ PRACTICE APOLOGIZING USING THESE SEVEN STEPS:

1. **Admit mistake:** "I know I was wrong when I . . ."

2. **Explain why it occurred:** "I was not being considerate . . ."

3. **Acknowledge hurting feelings:** "I realize I hurt your feelings."

4. **Apologize:** "I'm sorry I hurt your feelings."

5. **Affirm relationship:** "I still want to be your friend."

6. **Try to correct mistake:** "What can I do to make it up to you?"

7. **Adjust** yourself so you don't commit it again!

EXERCISE 16: What Makes You Angry?

Have your child circle his/her anger level for each of the following situations with one (1) being only slightly angry and six (6) being extremely angry.

Not very angry					very angry
1	2	3	4	5	6

Someone tells on you

1	2	3	4	5	6

You want a toy and don't get it

1	2	3	4	5	6

A friend doesn't invite you to a party

1	2	3	4	5	6

A friend breaks your toy

1	2	3	4	5	6

No one wants to play with you

1	2	3	4	5	6

You are accused of something you didn't do

1	2	3	4	5	6

You lose money

1	2	3	4	5	6

Not very angry					very angry
1	**2**	**3**	**4**	**5**	**6**

You do something well and no one notices

1	2	3	4	5	6

Someone teases you

1	2	3	4	5	6

You're told you can't join a game

1	2	3	4	5	6

Someone gets you in trouble

1	2	3	4	5	6

Your parents make you do chores

1	2	3	4	5	6

You don't get to do what you want

1	2	3	4	5	6

You don't do well at school or in a sport

1	2	3	4	5	6

EXERCISE 17: Handing Anger Differently

Have your child consider how he/she would like to handle these situations. Discuss their solutions.

1. Someone takes your toy

2. Someone teases you

3. Someone calls you a name

4. Someone cuts in front of you in line

5. Someone doesn't let you join in a game

6. _____

7. _____

8. _____

REVIEW STEPS:

1. **Identify feelings:** What am I feeling? Am I jealous? Scared? Hurt?

2. **Did the person intend to hurt me?**

3. **Reappraise beliefs** "He's out of control."

4. **What are my choices?** Fight back? Retreat? Think about it.

5. **Step back,** leave the room, take five deep breaths

6. **Consider choices:** leaving, saying something, ignoring it

7. **Choose best option.**

Conclusion

Learning Social Skills Is a Life-long Process

For children who have trouble processing information, going through this manual one time will not be enough repetition for them to learn all of the skills. They need to practice these skills in real life situations throughout their childhood. The goal of this manual is to help you as a parent define the social elements that are problematic for your child.

It would be naïve to think that all of these skills can be learned by all children in a short period of time. Perseveration, failing to show interest, being pushy, using tone and body language inappropriately are acquired as habits over time. They need to be unlearned while substituting new skills. However, without acquiring a different self-perception, new skills cannot be learned and retained.

The first change parents observe is that their children seem to be more mindful of their behavior. They may not yet have sufficient impulse control necessary to stop themselves from interrupting, but they now have a new awareness that they did interrupt. Parents need to appreciate that altering self-perception is the foundation for creating new behaviors. It should be positively reinforced. While parents may be impatient for more concrete changes to occur, seeing their behavior accurately is a very significant change.

Parents are encouraged to seek out trained professionals to help their children learn these skills. When children are in structured *ADDept* Social Skills Groups, the parents' role is far easier. Rather than having to teach the skills and monitor the progress, the parents' role switches to giving positive support and feedback, while helping their children structure social activities.

Parents are encouraged to enroll their children in *ADDept* Groups. To find out the availability of groups in your area, or to set up *ADDept* groups at your local elementary school, visit Dr. Giler's website at http://www.ld-add.com.

Appendices:

Parenting Website and References

APPENDIX A: What Is Attention Deficit Hyperactivity Disorder and How is it Diagnosed?

Attention Deficit Hyperactivity Disorder (ADHD) is most often an organic problem. ADHD is characterized by the inability to sustain focused attention (distractibility or inattention). To diagnose ADHD, mental health professionals ask parents and teachers to observe children and rate their behavior using specific questionnaires or checklists. These checklists rate the following behaviors which are present in most people with ADHD:

Distractibility

Inattention

Free flight of ideas (free associations to any other idea)

Impulsivity — Moodiness

Insatiability

Bursts of hot temper

Hyperactivity

In most cases, these behaviors were noticed before the child was seven years old. Since the ADHD person's ability to stay focused gets worse when the environment is noisy or full of distractions, teachers often are the first ones to notice when children are having trouble paying attention.

There are two major subtypes, ADHD with hyperactivity and ADHD without hyperactivity (inattentive form).

ADHD, with hyperactivity is often easier to diagnose as these children move continuously, have trouble sitting still, have poor impulse control, and may have temper outbursts more frequently than their peers.

ADHD, Inattentive type is often misdiagnosed. These children:

- may be withdrawn or "spaced-out" (may be more prevalent in girls)

127

- may be poor academic achievers

- may occur concurrently with Learning Disabilities

- may demonstrate excessive anxiety or shyness

We now know that ADHD can be concurrent with Learning Disabilities. Current research suggests anywhere from 25–50% of the people diagnosed with ADHD also have Learning Disabilities.

Is ADHD a Learning Disability?

It is clear that having ADHD can affect your ability to learn in a highly stimulating environment such as a noisy classroom due to the amount of auditory and visual distractions. However, ADHD is not a learning disability, per se. If children function at least one and a half to two years below grade level as the result of ADHD, the same criteria for services for children with Learning Disabilities applies as well (meaning they are eligible for special services under IDEA). One reason people think ADHD is a learning disability is that many children and adults have a Learning Disability along with their ADHD.

Evaluation for ADHD

1. **History:** A health professional should take a comprehensive family history. It needs to include when you first noticed a problem. Since assessment is based on the presence of these symptoms before the age of seven, particular attention needs to be paid to children's pre-school and early elementary school experiences.

2. **Identifying other family members with ADHD.** Does anyone else in your family have ADHD? We frequently find parents can identify another family member who has ADHD. Does a parent, sibling, or an aunt, uncle, cousin or grandparent suffer from undiagnosed ADHD? One way of recognizing undiagnosed ADHD is to look at the behavior patterns. Did this relative have an inconsistent job history?

Did this person have problems with his/her temper or was he/she dependent on drugs or alcohol? Many adults who have untreated ADHD have suffered with these problems.

3. **Behavior Checklists.** After consulting a medical doctor or psychologist, the parents and classroom teachers are asked to fill-out behavior checklists. These are standardized lists that look for typical ADHD behaviors. Sometimes, achievement tests are used in addition to checklists.

4. **Psychological tests** are sometimes used to define the scope of the problem. Because they can be costly, they are not always used.

5. **Medication trials.** One way of defining the presence of ADHD is to see if a trial of medication gets rid of the major symptoms. Many parents and adults have noticed an immediate change in impulsivity, hyperactivity or moodiness from medications. Medication trials are regulated by medical doctors.

6. **Continuous Performance Tests:** IVA, TOVA, and CPT. Continuous performance tests are a popular means of assessment. Although the creators of the tests say they aren't to be used as a sole means for assessing ADHD, many clinicians are using them in this way.

The major problem with these tests is they don't take into account the children taking the test may have Learning Disabilities that affect eye-hand coordination. So, when these children push a button slowly in response to a letter which has flashed on the computer screen or a sound they have heard, are they really inattentive? Maybe they have trouble responding and evaluating what they have seen or heard or just have difficulty with their finger responding to their brain's command. To accurately assess ADHD, the makers of these continuous performance tests have to create a database of Learning Disabled children and adults. Until they do, these are not valid assessment tools for anyone who has ADHD and Learning Disabilities (which may be 25-50% of the ADHD population).

A positive use for these tests is to demonstrate increased attention or shorter response time. In other words, children should take the test before starting a treatment regime and then take it again after their treatments and compare the results. The effects of any treatment can be measured in this way: medication trials, training in EEG biofeedback, or sensory-motor integration therapy.

Warning:

Do not diagnose yourself or your child. See a competent medical doctor, psychologist, school psychologist or psychotherapist who is familiar with ADHD. CHADD, the support group for children and adults with ADHD, has a list of all of its active, clinical members.

APPENDIX B: What Are Learning Disabilities?

Learning Disabilities are due to an organic problem (about 90%) which affects one's ability to use or process language or other symbol systems (such as mathematics). These disabilities can interfere with how your child processes written or spoken language. Dyslexia is the most common form of Learning Disability. Dyslexia (dys = cannot, lexia = words) affects how well your child can read, write, or spell.

The other kinds of Learning Disabilities affect:

speech

reading

writing

hearing

organization

memory

coordination

reading nonverbal expressions

An important part of the national definition put forth by the National Joint Committee on Learning Disabilities is that these disabilities are noted by:

> . . . significant difficulties in the acquisition and use of listening, speaking, reading, writing, reasoning, or mathematical abilities. These disorders are intrinsic to the individual and presumed due to central nervous system dysfunction (1995).

If a child is functioning 1–2 years below grade level, you can request that he or she be tested for Learning Disabilities by going to your local public school and submitting your request in writing. Since children with Learning Disabilities are entitled to remedial help under federal law 94:142 (IDEA), your local public school must test children to see if they qualify for services.

Possible school-based services can include:

- tutoring (in class or in a pull-out program) with reading, spelling, writing or math

- speech therapy

- adaptive physical education

- psychological counseling

- classroom accommodations

- use of assistive technology

- books on audiotape, a service provided by the organization, Recording for the Blind and Dyslexic

- programs that train auditory skills

If your child qualifies for services, you will have a meeting to set up your child's Individual Educational Program (IEP). At the IEP meeting the following people should be present: your child's teacher, his/her principal, the school psychologist, the resource person, and one or both parents. The purpose of this meeting is for the school to define the course of action it plans to take to help your child master his/her deficiencies. It should include a summary of your child's testing results, annual goals for your child, and a *description of the services* (tutoring, speech therapy, adaptive physical education, etc) that the school plans to provide for your child.

Evaluation for Learning Disabilities. Testing for learning problems is usually done by a psychologist. Children are tested for I.Q. (if allowed in your state) or ability. Ability is compared to your child's academic performance. When a child performs at least 1.5 years below his or her ability, he or she should be tested for specific Learning Disabilities. The tests can include:

Standard achievement tests

I.Q. or performance tests

Specific tests to measure memory, sequencing, auditory, visual or motor

Children who have severe Learning Disabilities are usually evaluated while in elementary school. School districts focus on the children who are performing below grade level. Boys are diagnosed more frequently than girls, and minorities are often not properly assessed due to the presumption that the problem is due to insufficient exposure.

Advocacy groups, such as TASK, Team of Advocates for Special Kids, can answer any further specific questions which you might have. You can call them at (714) 533-8275 or email them at taskca@aol.com.

APPENDIX C: Treatments for ADHD/LD

ADHD/LD problems can affect many areas of your child's life:

- Self-esteem

- Academic Skills

- Social Relationships

- Family relationships

The treatment needs to be multi-faceted and can include:

- Psycho-Education

- Medication (including herbs and homeopathic drugs)

- Behavioral therapies

- Social Skills

- Organization and/or time management

- Remedial help for academic deficits

- EEG Biofeedback for improved concentration and stress reduction

- Family therapy

- Individual therapy

1. Psycho-Education

Parents and children need to understand the scope of the problem. ADHD/LD problems can affect your child socially, emotionally, and behaviorally. As a parent, seek out information. The parents' job is complex and requires that you:

- Know what the problem is and understand how it affects your child and family

- Know what your child's special gifts are

- Have realistic expectations of your child e.g. know the difference between lack of cooperation and inability

- Have a working discipline strategy

- Know what remedial help your child needs and where to get it

- Know the laws that protect your child

- Know how to have fun with your family

2. Parenting class

   Although children with ADHD/LD have unique problems, many of the general parenting principles apply to them as well. They particularly need predictable discipline and consequences, as well as a fairly consistent structure.

3. Behavioral Therapies

   The most effective treatments for ADHD/LD are behavioral interventions. They include:

   - Organization and time management

   - Family therapy focusing on structure and management strategies

   - Individual therapy focusing on changing behaviors

   - Social skills training for children — e.g. the *ADDept Social Skills Curriculum*

   - Physical activities or therapies that focus on coordination and sequencing

4. School-based interventions:

   Children who qualify as LD or who perform 1.5-2 years below their grade level can receive some of these services through public schools:

- Remedial help with reading, spelling, math, organization, coordination

- Speech therapy

- Adaptive Physical Education or Occupational Therapy

- Counseling

- Instruction in assistive technology

5. Social Skills Training

   Many children with ADHD/LD problems are deficient in social skills. Because they have not attended to or comprehended the more subtle rules of communication, they frequently make mistakes and are teased by the other children.

6. Medications

APPENDIX D: Parenting Skills: How to Manage Your ADHD/LD Child

Do you feel you are failing as a parent? Take heart, you aren't alone. Having ADHD/LD children stresses the best child-parent relationship. Why? ADHD/LD children have a very difficult time following multi-step directions, listening, and finishing tasks. Their moodiness can be hard to handle. As the parent, you are frequently in the role of correcting or reminding your children, or are dealing with guilt because of your lack of patience or short temper. Or you may feel shame because you are frequently disappointed with them. Many ADHD/LD children require "high maintenance." Much of the family interaction time (and energy) is centered around their needs. It's no wonder that many parents feel they are doing a poor job.

The treatment for ADHD/LD is complex. As the parent, you need to make many choices. You need to become an informed consumer and beware of people who try to sell you a "quick fix."

1. KNOW THE SCOPE OF THE PROBLEM

   Parents and children need to understand the scope of the problem. ADHD/LD problems can affect your child socially, emotionally, and behaviorally.

   The parents' job is complex and requires that you:

   • Know what the problem is and understand how it affects your child and your family.

   • Know what your child's special gifts are.

2. HAVE REALISTIC EXPECTATIONS

   Parents need to know both their children's strengths and weaknesses. They also need to know what behaviors are under their children's conscious control and which

139

behaviors are not. Defining the difference between inability and non-compliance is one of the hardest tasks for parents. Once you see what your child can or cannot do, then you are ready to form a discipline strategy.

To define non-compliance, answer this question: can your child control the identified behavior? If the answer is yes, is your child choosing to disobey? If the answer is yes, you are defining non-compliance. However, for many ADHD/LD children, a behavior can be inability even if it there are times when the child can control the behavior. Let's take movement as an example. Sometimes, when a child is highly interested or scared, he/she can control their need to move. Since the parent sees that this control of movement some of the time, the parent assumes the child can control their need to move all of the time. This is incorrect.

Many ADHD children use movement to wake up their brain, moving helps them pay attention. However, many parents view their child's squirming as an act of defiance instead of a behavior which they have trouble controlling. If you think your child is defying you, you might get angry. However, if you view movement as an inability, you might choose to ignore it or to teach your child to move in ways which don't bother people. In most cases, movement in ADHD children is an inability and not an act of defiance.

As you can see, this distinction is important because to manage inability effectively, you ignore it. To manage non-compliance, you use discipline. If you are having trouble with this concept, you aren't alone. This topic is one of the key concepts in Dr. Giler's parenting class.

3. HAVE A DISCIPLINE STRATEGY

One of the most important things you can do for your child is to be consistent. Children with ADHD/LD learn more slowly than other children. Having predictable consequences helps them learn. There are many behavioral methods one can use to form a discipline strategy, and most parenting classes talk about how to discipline your child. Two basic principles are to be consistent and to use less emotion.

There are many methods one can use to reinforce "start" behaviors. Behavioral charting and the use of rewards are probably the best ways to let your children know what you expect of them and what will occur if they do not behave.

Disciplining teenagers is more complicated. Teenagers need to be part of the process or they tend to rebel. You need to include your teenager in the planning of consequences for misbehaviors. We discuss ways to manage teenagers in the third class, Disciplining Your ADHD/LD Child.

APPENDIX E: Assistive Technology

Assistive Technology refers to the whole range of computers, tape recorders and other gadgets which help people with Learning Disabilities compensate for some of their weaker areas such as spelling, math, or problems with reading or writing. We will discuss a few technologies that can be beneficial. By no means is this an exhaustive list of technologies. For a more complete list, the reader is referred to Dr. Marshall Raskind's pamphlet entitled *Assistive Technology for Children with Learning Difficulties*. To order a copy, contact the Parents' Education Resource Center at (800) 471-9545.

Speech Recognition refers to computer software programs that are programmed to recognize your voice . You read designated text into a microphone which your computer stores as speech files. When you want to write, you talk into a microphone in either a slightly halted manner, or a natural speaking voice. The computer then types out your spoken words as text using correct spelling. While the technology isn't perfect, in that it can mis-hear words, it is a great help to those who have problems with writing because of spelling problems, processing problems, or typing.

Three companies which manufacture these programs are DragonDictate (Discreet and Naturally Speaking), Kurzweil (a Xerox product) and IBM. Most of these programs are for IBM compatible computers and need a pentium 2 or 3 processor with a speed of 400 mega hertz or better and a minimum of 128 meg of RAM, a soundblaster soundcard, and a minimum of 300 megs of available hard drive space. These programs are available through many discount office supply stores.

A side benefit of speech recognition is that it appears to be teaching children to spell and write better.

Optical Character Recognition (OCR) is the opposite of speech recognition. The computer takes written text and turns it into spoken language. In other words, it reads to you. Unfortunately, it is also much more expensive and requires a lot more technology than just a computer, sound card, and a microphone. You need a scanner, computer with sufficient memory and hard drive space, and the software program. It is perfect technology for the very slow reader who wants to read more complicated text. The problem (other than the cost), is that the voice quality is somewhat mechanical. This will probably improve over the next few years. Some companies selling OCR systems include Humanware, Arkenstone and Zerox/Kurzweil.

Two writing programs which are appropriate for elementary aged children are by Don Johnson *Co: Writer* (a word prediction program) and *Write: Outloud,* a talking word processing program. These programs work on Apple computers.

Computer Flow Charts turn your ideas into a picture or flow chart, referred to as mapping. Programs which do mapping provide a great tool for visual learners who are having trouble outlining or organizing their ideas. The program allows you to add ideas and then move them around or change topics to which they are linked. With a stroke of a key, you turn your diagram into an organized flow chart or an outline.

Spelling Checkers have been around for a while. There is a pocket version as well as programs which are embedded in most word processing programs.

Remedial Technology

While most of the technologies mentioned here are compensatory, there is a new remedial technology worth investigating: computer programs for auditory processing problems. Ninety percent of the Learning Disabled population is dyslexic and about 67% of this group are dysphonetic, meaning they have trouble distinguishing phonological groups or sounds. Dr. Tallal has developed a computer program that expands sounds. This is a computer program which looks like a computer game, but helps children to recognize sounds. The sounds are then progressively shortened until they resemble normal speech. While the research on this method isn't new, the *Fastforword* program is fairly new (about 2 years old). It is only sold to educational and speech therapists. Last year, they came out with *Fastforward 2* that extends the training. However, you have to do *Fastforward 1* to do *Fastforward 2*.

Its major drawback is that it is expensive (about $3,000 for a six week treatment). If you do the program as a home study course, you can reduce the cost to $1200 to $1500, depending on how the therapist structures the fee. There isn't a great deal of independent research yet, so the impressive results that Tallal have obtained may be biased. We certainly do not believe her claim that this program is for everyone. However, we think it shows a lot of promise as an early remediation for children with auditory processing problems, specifically children who have difficulty repeating sounds or sequences of sounds.

Another program on the market is *Earobics*. This is an auditory program that helps children hear phonological sounds more clearly. It doesn't expand the sound (as the computer assisted *Fastforward* program does), however, the cost is substantially less (about $300). Many school districts have purchased this program.

For more current information go to http://www.ld-add.com/Tech.htm

APPENDIX F: REFERENCES

Achenbach, T. and Edelbrock, C. (1983). *Manual For The Child Behavior Checklist And Revised Child Behavior Profile*. Burlington, VT: University of Vermont, Department of Psychiatry.

Armstrong, T. (1987). *In Their Own Way: Discovering and Encouraging Your Child's Personal Learning Style*. New York: Putnam & Sons.
Author sees some Learning Disabilities resulting from a mismatch of child's learningstyle and the way in which information is taught. Includes some useful exercises.

Ayers, A.J. (1972). *Sensory integration and learning disorders*. Los Angeles, CA: Western Psychological Services.

Barkley, R. A. (1990). *Attention-Deficit Hyperactivity Disorder: A Handbook For Diagnosis And Treatment*. New York: Guilford Press.
Excellent workbook for parents and therapists.

Borenstein, S. & Radman, Z. (1984). *Learning to Learn: An Approach to Study Skills*. Dubuque, IO: Kendall/Hunt Publishing Co.
A very good study skills book. May be out of print.

Cohen-Posey, K. (1995). *How To Handle Bullies, Teasers and Other Meanies*. Rainbow Books.
Useful book for children ages 8–12. Recommended by American Library Association

Colvin, G., Ramsey, E., Walker, H.M., et. al (1995). *Antisocial Behavior in School : Strategies and Best Practices*. Pacific Grove, CA: Brooks/Cole Publishers. Technical, research based book.
Excellent resource for educators, psychologists and researchers who work with antisocial, oppositional children.

Community Alliance for Special Education (CASE) and Protection and Advocacy, Inc. (PAI) (1994). *Special Education Rights and Responsibilities*. San Francisco, CA. (415) 928-2273.
This book describes the federal laws and how they apply to the schools.

Cratty, Bryant, Goldman, Richard L. (Editors). *Learning Disabilities: Contemporary Viewpoints*. Netherlands: Harwood Academic Publishers.
Very good book for those interested in current research.

Davis, L., Sirotowitz, S. and Parker, H.C. (1996). *Study Strategies Made Easy: A Practical Plan for School Success*. ADD Warehouse.

Dockstader, M. & Payne, L. (1989). *To a Different Drummer: Helping Children with Learning Disabilities*. Albuquerque, N.M.: I.S.S. Publications
Remedial techniques for working with young children with learning problems.

Everett, C.A. and S. V. (1999). *Family Therapy for ADHD: Treating Children, Adolescents and Adults*. New York: Guilford Press.
The first book for therapists who are treating ADHD in families. Good therapeutic structure and goals. Recommended for practitioners.

Giler, J. Z. (1998). *ADDept Social Skills Curriculum: A ten week curriculum to teach 10 basic social skills and self evaluation to children with ADHD/LD problems*. Santa Barbara: CA.: CES Publications.

Goldstein, A. (1988). *The Prepare Curriculum: Teaching Prosocial Competencies*. Champaign, IL: Research Press.

Gresham, F.M. (1982a). "Misguided Mainstreaming: The Case For Social Skills Training With Handicapped Children." *Teaching Exceptional Children* 48:422–433. Reston, VA: Council for Exceptional Children.

Gresham, F.M. (1982b). *Social Skills: Principles, Practices And Procedures*. Des Moines, IA: Iowa Department of Public Instruction.

Gresham, F.M. (1990). "Best Practices In Social Skills Training." *Best Practices In School Psychology II*. (pp. 695-709). Thomas & Grimes (Eds.) Washington, DC: The National Association of School Psychologists.

Gresham, F.M. and Elliott, S.N. (1994). *Social Skills Rating System (Parent, Teacher And Student Forms And Manual)*. Circle Pines: MN: American Guidance Service.

Greene, R. W. (1999). *The Explosive Child : A New Approach for Understanding and Parenting Easily Frustrated*, 'Chronically Inflexible' Children (also audiotape)

Guevremont, D. (1990)."Social Skills and Peer Relationship Training." Barclay, R. A. (ed) *Attention-Deficit Hyperactivity Disorder: A Handbook For Diagnosis And Treatment*. New York: Guilford Press

Hallowell, E. & Ratey, J. J. (1994). *Driven to Distraction*. New York: Simon and Schuster.
One of my favorite overview books because of its great lists.

Kelly, K. & Ramundo, P. (1993). *You Mean I'm not Lazy, Stupid or Crazy?* Tyrell and Jeremy Press.

Lavoie, R. (1994). *Learning Disability And Social Skills: Last One Picked . . . First One Picked On*. Washington D.C.: WETA, PBS Video.

Lavoie, R. (1995). *Understanding Learning Disabilities: The FAT CITY Workshop.* Washington D.C.: WETA, PBS Video.

McGinnis, E., Goldstein, A., Sprafkin, R.P. & Gershaw, N.J. (1984). *Skillstreaming the Elementary School Child.* Champaign, Ill: Research Press Company.

Moss, Robert (1996). *Why Johnny Can't Concentrate.* New York: Bantam Books.

Nadeau, K. (1994). *Survival Guide for College Students with ADD or LD.* Magination Press.

Norwicki, S. & Duke, M.l (1992). *Helping the Child Who Doesn't Fit In.* Atlanta: GA. Good book for working with young children. Lists many exercises one can do with young children. Good for teachers and parents.

Parker, H. C. (1996). *Behavior Management At Home: A Token Economy Program for Children and Teens.* ADD Warehouse

Phelan, Thomas W. (1993). *Surviving Your Adolescents: A Vital Parents' Guide.* Glen Ellyn, Ill.: Child Management, Inc.

Phelan, T W. (video). *Magic 1, 2, 3.* Glen Ellyn, Ill.: Child Management, Inc. Good behavior management video for parents of 2–12 year olds.

Reif, S. F. (1993). *How to Reach and Teach ADD/ADHD Children. Practical Techniques, Strategies, and Interventions for Helping Children with Attention Problems and Hyperactivity.* West Nyack, NY: Center for Applied Research.

Roberts, C. A. and Elliott, P. T. (1995). *ADHD and Teens.* Texas: Taylor Publishing Co.

Smith, S. (1995). *No Easy Answers: The Learning Disabled Child at Home and at School.* N.Y.: Bantam Books

Solden, S. (1995). *Women with Attention Deficit Disorder.* Underwood Books One of the few books on how ADHD affects women.

Stevens, S. H. (1999). *The LD Child and the ADHD Child: Ways Parents and Professionals Can Help.*

Swanson, L., et. al. (1999). *Interventions for Students with Learning Disabilities: A Meta-Analysis of Treatment Outcomes.* New York: Guilford Publications.

Shure, M.B. (1992). *I Can Problem Solve: Intermediate Elementary Grades.* Champaign: IL: Research Press.

Silver, L. (1992). *The Misunderstood Child: Guide for Parents of Children with Learning Disabilities*. New York: McGraw Hill.
A good overview book on Learning Disabilities.

Thompson, Sue. (1998). *Nonverbal Learning Disabilities*. Santa Cruz, CA., Lingui-Systems.

Wagner, M., D'Amico, R., and Marder, C., et al. (1992). *What Happens Next? Trends In Post-School Outcomes Of Youth With Disability. The Second Comprehensive Report From The National Longitudinal Transition Study Of Special Education Students*. Menlo Park, CA: SRI International.

Walker, H.M., McConnell, S., and Holmes, D., Todis, B., Walker, J. and Golden, N. (1983). *The Walker Social skills curriculum: The ACCEPTS Program*. Austin, TX: PRO-Ed.

Whitham, C. (1991). *Win the Whining War and Other Skirmishes: A Family Peace Plan*. Los Angeles, CA.: Perspective Publishing

JANET Z. GILER, Ph.D.
California licensed Marriage and Family Therapist
MR 17332

For information about the *ADDept* Curriculum contact:

JANET Z. GILER, Ph.D., M.F.T.

30 W. Mission St. #5, Santa Barbara, CA 93101

(805) 563-2325

Fax (805) 687-1204

jzgiler@earthlink.net

Visit website http://www.ADDept.org

C.E.S. ORDER FORM

Janet Z. Giler, Ph.D.
549 N. Hope Ave.
Santa Barbara, CA 93110

To order by fax 805-687-1204

Package #01	**Professional Package** *ADDept Social Skills Curriculum,* "From Acting Out to Fitting In," Instructional video, and 4 workbooks. Starter kit 2–4 Kits, 20% off; 4–7 kits, 30% off; more than 8 kits, 35% off	$295.00
Package #02	*ADDept Social Skills Workbook for Children* 8–13 years old. Only sold to trainers. 5 @ $45, 10 @ $80	5 @ $45 10 @ $80
Package #03	*Socially ADDept: A Manual for Parents*	$ 29.95

Stock #	Description	Quantity	Price

Shipping
Add $5 for orders under $50;
Add $10 for over $50, Add $10 for
orders over $100 and $15 for the
ADDept Curriculum Starter Kit

California Residents: Tax %7.75 _____

Shipping _____

Total _____

Name: _____   Email: _____

Address: _____   City: _____

State: _____   Zip: _____

Phone: _____   Fax _____

❑ Mastercard   ❑ Visa   ❑ Check

Account Number: _____ Exp.: _____

Signature: _____